Advance Praise

"Emmet has a unique view into how to successfully grow a DSO. I've been lucky to witness his strong leadership in multiple organizational structures. He's helped me understand the challenges and opportunities particular to group dentistry. Emmet's advice and expertise is much sought after by our members, the DSO Secrets podcast/Facebook community, as well as the group dentistry industry as a whole. 'When Emmet talks, you listen.' He's made quite a positive impact in leading group dentistry forward, keeping quality care first. I am excited to have a book with his thoughts and strategies for reference!"

—**Jacob Puhl,** CEO & Partner of Dentist Entrepreneur Organization

"You'll be inspired by his practical approach. You'll be moved to action by his tips."

—**Margaret McGuckin,** Co-Founder of i3 Ignite

"DSOs have long been the fastest growing portion of a huge sector in our economy. A codification of the hard-won lessons and a look at how to prepare for the future are long overdue to help us all better meet the needs of providers and their patients. This book is one of the first resources that finally accomplishes that, and there is no better person to create it than Emmet."

—**Steven C. Bilt,** Co-Founder & CEO of Smile Brands

"As an entrepreneur, I've realized that the dental space is one of the most difficult spaces to figure out and do well. This book is, finally, the handbook to make it a little easier."

—**Dr. AJ Acierno,** DDS, Chief Operating Officer of Smile Brands Inc. and CEO of DecisionOne Dental

"Emmet does an amazing job spelling out how to build your dental company. This book will help you anticipate and be prepared for the challenges and hurdles that a dental entrepreneur will face. I'm very grateful and fortunate that Emmet is willing to share his knowledge and experience."

—**Marc Farber,** CEO & Founder of Edge Dental Management, DEO Member

"After many years of working in the DSO space, I have found Emmet to be one of the most dynamic thought leaders of the industry. He brings a genuine, honest, and relatable mindset to the challenges we all face every day."

—**Ken Cooper,** Co-Founder of North American Dental Group

"This book is certain to be life-changing. It will make you think out of the box. Emmet is a true force in our industry. I highly recommend you read this book ASAP and put the thought process into place. There are books, and then there are those that will speak to you. This will speak to you! DO NOT MISS IT!!"

—**Dee Fischer,** Founder of Fischer's Professional Group

"I've worked closely with Emmet and witnessed his thoughtful and unique approach to building a successful DSO, with a focus on the well-being and satisfaction of its patients, team members, and doctors. Through building relationships with other experts in the field, he has identified the most glaring needs in our industry today and built a roadmap for success that we can all follow."

—**Dr. Nieku Manshadi,** Pediatric Dentist & Co-Founder of OrthoDent

"Emmet's passion for the DSO industry is abundant. He consistently works to help others succeed and delivers on his commitment to support dentists so they can focus on providing excellent patient care. I have no doubt that this book will help others in the DSO space."

—**Scotte Hudsmith,** Co-Founder & Chairman of Smile Doctors

"I've witnessed Emmet's unique skill and passion on how to build a DSO. I am excited for this book to give some guidance from his experience and leadership skills to the dental community."

—**Norma Romero,** Chief Compliance Officer of Community Dental Partners

"Emmet is one of the unique entrepreneurs who has not only built a thriving business from scratch but also contributed to the dental industry through various efforts. I have had the privilege of watching him grow both personally and professionally over the past ten years. He understands the dynamics of how to build and scale a dental office as well as how to scale the business side. Emmet has sat on both sides of the table, and that's what makes his perspective differentiated."

—**Dr. Sulman Ahmed**, D.M.D., CEO & Founder of Deca Dental Group

"When built correctly, DSOs can be a huge support to clinicians to increase their autonomy to provide better patient care. Now we have a book to show us how to build a great DSO."

—**Dr. Craig Copeland**, DDS, Chief Dental Officer
of Community Dental Partners

"Emmet is not only a great person but a great leader as well. I was able to experience it first hand when he took over as president of the ADSO. Emmet was able to deal with unprecedented circumstances (COVID pandemic) and rebuild the organization during its most challenging time. I know he has approached building his successful DSO in the very same way. I'm excited to have a book with his thoughts and strategies."

—**Dr. Michael Riccobene**, DDS, CEO of Riccobene Associates

"Emmet Scott is the most connected man in the DSO industry. He's genuine, he's knowledgeable, and he understands this complex business. If anybody should be writing the book on DSOs, it's him. It's about time!"

—**Dr. Eric J. Roman**, DDS Executive Coach for DSO Leaders

"Emmet is one of the few people that has touched all aspects of the dental industry. From supporting clinicians, leading executive meetings, serving on DSO boards, doing thought-provoking podcasts, and partnering with emerging DSOs. Emmet has a unique view on how to successfully grow DSOs that I have always found to be helpful. I've witnessed Emmet's strong leadership in multiple organizational structures, and I am excited to have a book with his thoughts and strategies. It's great to see this come together—it will be immensely valuable to all dental leaders."

—**Doug Brown**, Vice Chairman of Affordable Care LLC

"Emmet is a thought leader in this industry and has the unique ability of distilling down information to the most important points. His insight will help you and your leadership team get clarity quickly and prepare your company for future growth."

—**Jodi Evans**, CVO & Founder of Revolutionary Tribes

"I applaud Emmet's mission to create a community where dental entrepreneurs have a voice and way to succeed. Through his book, he is speaking to and creating the next generation of DSO leaders."

—Dr. Maryam Beyramian, DDS, MBA, CEO & Co-Founder
of Westwind Integrated Health

"Emmet's work within the dental industry has been nothing short of extraordinary. From building out their own unique dental concept to scaling to become one of the largest DSO's in the nation, Emmet has always put the patient and his team first. His style of servant leadership combined with a practical approach to growth is an inspiration for anyone who aspires to build their own dental empire."

—Dustin Netral, President & CEO of Vista Verde Dental Partners

"In this book Emmet does a great job of balancing all the mindsets I've needed as an entrepreneur and as an executive to grow and build a great DSO, as well as many of the tactical things that any emerging DSO needs to know."

—Dr. Dhaval Thakkar, DMD, CEO & Founder of 3C Dental Group

"'You can do this,' DSO Secrets takes the mystery out of building a DSO. Emmet's book is a how-to that will give you a roadmap and the confidence to build your own future success!"

—Dr. Jeff Moos, CEO & President of Moos-e "Your Business Elevated"

"Emmet says, 'DSOs will only be successful to the extent they provide support to the clinicians.' I couldn't agree more!"

—**Dr. Kyle Ramond,** OrthoDent

"Emmet highlights in his book the various benefits to DSOs. Healthcare is a very complex environment. DSOs support providers in navigating and deliver additional resources to help dentists as they deliver care."

—**Dr. Andrew Matta,** Chief Medical Officer of North American Dental Group

"Everyone who started a DSO or has worked in the DSO industry at one point wished there was someone to guide them and give them not just the 'dos' but also the 'don'ts.' Even though we all learn and grow from our early mistakes, it's always better to have someone guide you through to avoid some very expensive mistakes, especially when solutions can be simple. Emmet has grown a DSO in a very competitive market along with assembling a team of current and future leaders. In this book, Emmet has shared several gems that can be of tremendous help for a dentist starting a DSO, an entrepreneur, or an executive trying to navigate through many lectical and strategic issues to scale or to just manage an existing DSO well."

—**Dr. Aman Kaur,** CEO of AiM Dental Alliance,
Founder & President of Women in DSO

"Emmet has an incredible vision for growth in the dental industry and a remarkable way of communicating his vision and inspiring others to rise to the challenge. He believes dental should be at the forefront of the healthcare industry, and this book serves as a clear outline for anyone who shares his passion."

—**Amber Nish**, Chief Marketing Officer at Community Dental Partners

"I've witnessed Emmet's strong leadership in multiple situations, from marketing and finance to culture and how to challenge directly while also making someone feel like they've just been awarded the gold medal. It's like when he starts talking you feel like you're listening to a TED Talk and are hanging on every word while also jotting down some great thoughts he's shared. I am excited to finally have a book with his thoughts and strategies and can't wait for the next edition!"

—**Jackie Brown**, Executive Director of Human Resources at Community Dental Partners

"Having experienced Emmet's leadership first hand across multiple organizations, I am excited to have a book with his thoughts and strategies. He has this way of teaching as he speaks as well as asking the right questions to push you in your thoughts. I'm blessed to work with him."

—**Andrea Grice**, Executive Director of Facilities at Community Dental Partners

"The insights and wisdom found in DSO Secrets *are exactly what the dental industry needs today. I highly recommend this book to anyone that is wanting to grow in the DSO space."*

—**Brett Evans**, Director of Strategic Planning at Community Dental Partners

"I have personally witnessed Emmet's ability to distill complexity into simplicity, coupled with his desire to connect and engage at a deep personal level. It has been an honor to work with him and learn from him. I can't wait to get my hands on this book!"

—**Michael Irving**, Chief Technology Officer at Community Dental Partners

DSO
SECRETS

DSO

SECRETS

THE ULTIMATE GUIDE TO BUILDING
YOUR **DENTAL EMPIRE**

EMMET SCOTT

DEO DENTAL MEDIA PUBLISHING

DSO SECRETS
The Ultimate Guide to Building Your Dental Empire

ISBN	978-1-5445-2604-1	*Hardcover*
	978-1-5445-2603-4	*Paperback*
	978-1-5445-2602-7	*Ebook*
	978-1-5445-2605-8	*Audiobook*

Contents

Foreword

Emmet Scott and I have been best friends since we were two years old. He had a front seat to a childhood that guided me toward dentistry—by way of racing adventures. My father was a passionate auto mechanic, especially in service of all things fast. Based out of our fully equipped backyard garage, my father fixed and flipped cars, built and raced dune buggies, and even flew planes. I loved every minute and was right there with him, racing and tinkering and adventuring.

Of course, airplanes, dune buggies, and the racing life need underwriting. Looking around, my father discovered a growing need for dental techs to support the dental industry. He built his own dental lab and soon became a premier provider in the small but booming town of Henderson, Nevada.

Like the vehicles, the dental lab was a childhood fixture for me. I began working in it by the time I was eleven years old. By fourteen, I was doing the waxing and metal works. By sixteen, I delivered finished products to dental practices and interacted with staff and doctors. By eighteen, I performed high-end ceramic work. Dentistry and lab work were at the core of my teenage development. I was a lab tech by day, mechanic by night, racing vehicles whenever time allowed.

Now I, like my father before me, had to make a decision: how would I fund my vehicle and adventure passion? I'd need a substantial income, but I'd also need time to actually enjoy my hobby. The answer seemed obvious. I'd interacted with a lot of dentists delivering products from my father's lab. They were wealthy and worked three days a week. They seemed to have plenty of cash and time for their hobbies, the very combination I was looking for. And I'd grown up around dentistry. It seemed the natural choice.

In dental school, where my background gave me an advantage, it seemed the right choice too. But the world of dentistry was changing. Dental school professors didn't prepare me or my fellow students for the massive shift happening in the industry. When I graduated in 2005, I was unprepared for the new reality. Blindsided, I soon faced the real potential of bankruptcy. Nothing was going as it had been modeled in my youth by those successful dentists living the life.

It had to be me, I thought. I was doing something wrong. I'd planned to have my own office up and running within one to two years. By year two, I thought I'd have a hired associate to work a second office I would have opened. I'd be working just a few days a week as I watched the money roll in. It was the story I'd heard from every other college student and professor feeding the dream.

You probably heard that story too. And, like me, you've probably come to realize that nowadays you can't just be a dentist. You have to be a dentist and a businessperson. I began educating myself, reading books about business development, systemizing processes, and leadership. As I studied in the harsh light of day, I saw the realities of just what it would take to achieve those multiple practices. I learned one very important lesson: humility. I needed help.

I realized that while I'd been in dental school learning everything I could about dental health, somewhere else someone else was learning about scaling healthcare practices. Someone else was learning about marketing. Someone else was learning about technology. We were all learning our chosen industries with the same focus and intensity. In other words, just like someone else couldn't scratch the surface of what I know about dentistry, I could never scratch the surface of entrepreneurship and business.

Fortunately, I knew a very successful entrepreneur, my best friend from the age of two, Emmet Scott.

When I called Emmet, I was working as an associate but ready to try again—to open up my own practice, one focused on children's dentistry. I felt nervous. My previous attempt to open a practice had almost resulted in financial failure. I hoped Emmet's business and entrepreneurial abilities would prevent a repeat.

I asked him to help me design a business plan so I could have the right elements in place to make everything run smoothly. Emmet looked at my practice as an entrepreneur and businessperson. He knew I had a passion for serving the underserved in my community, I loved kids (I have seven of them), and I was fluent in Spanish, as I'd served a two-year mission in Chile. He took my idea of a children-focused practice and organized it around a storybook concept under the brand Smile Magic. His insights helped me provide the best care and patient experience to my underserved Hispanic community of little ones.

We launched. While I focused on doing what I did best around clinical standards of care, Emmet took care of the business end—the marketing strategy, the organization chart, the technology challenges—all the business components that would allow my practice to thrive as my patients thrived. And he wasn't doing it alone. He was building an entire team to support me.

In actuality, he was creating the basis for a DSO. How'd that work out for me? Well, through our DSO, I now support over sixty locations and several brands. I have a full executive team supporting me and more locations we are building or associating with. Emmet helped me scale, and scaling means that over the last ten years I've positively impacted millions of patient lives. Not many dentists can say that.

I have what we all wanted, dreamed of, and hoped for in dental school: a lucrative career, a successful practice, freedom of time, and a huge impact in our communities. I've always had an entrepreneurial spirit. With Emmet's involvement, my entrepreneurial desires have been fulfilled.

I'm so glad to have had a friend with this capability—the capability to teach me to become the dentist-entrepreneur I wanted to be. To help me scale up my business to make such a difference in not only my life but also the lives of those in my community.

And I'm glad Emmet is willing and able to share with you everything he's done for me, everything he has learned about scaling up and DSOs, with his new best friends: each of you.

Dr. E. Chad Evans,
Clinical Chair of Community Dental Partners

Introduction

My friend Chad's experience trying to get a dental practice going and then scale up the success is typical nowadays. It used to be that emerging from dental school was a golden ticket to life. Back then, the rules and regulations capped the number of dentists in a given area and made most marketing illegal. The marketing rules were so tight that dental boards would often measure a dentist's name on their door nameplate to make sure it measured no more than two inches. Meanwhile, caps on the number of dentists able to practice in the same area ensured that each had plenty of business. The dentists didn't fear competition. In fact, they could refer patients to each other without a care. They really did have a golden ticket. All they had to do was cash it in.

But traditional capitalism was coming in to overturn all that. Sometime around the turn of the twenty-first century, the dental industry experienced a fundamental shift along with the rest of the world—the internet was coming. Deregulation, increased access to more information, and entitlement to convenience slammed every industry. Customers wanted things to be easy and fast, and they had lots of choices to select from.

This trend continues today. Every dentist's biggest competitor is the myriad of choices customers now have to spend their time, attention, and money on. Unprepared, many flounder. Dentists who used to work three days a week in a bubble outside capitalism could make $400,000 to $500,000 annually. The new reality has many dentist-owners who work five days a week earning an average yearly income of about $150,000.

What a shock! They'd expected to emerge from school with a golden ticket. Now they emerge burdened with student loan debt into a world that has, unbeknownst to them, changed the rules of the game.

To ramp things up, to have the income and freedom, dentists were going to have to learn a new game of marketing and customer satisfaction, and, for the most ambitious, the ability to open additional practices, hire associates, and build entire company support systems. But how? And what does it cost?

A lot. The entrepreneurial journey that lets dentists scale up to increase income and freedom isn't quick, and a wrong turn can leave you out of resources to go forward. A lot of would-be entrepreneurs get stuck, maybe at a level that would seem promising if only they knew exactly how to break through to the success and lifestyle they envisioned.

All they want is a good living without having to stay bent over someone's teeth every day for the rest of their professional lives, but the intensity of doing it—of doing it all to have it all— is burning them out.

Where you're at requires so much that you know you can't keep suffering this intensity overload forever. We are more than twenty years past that day when the internet launched to the public and created major shifts in the dental industry, and yet dentists are still graduating with a degree that prepares them to care for others' health but not the health of their practices and doesn't prepare them to scale their impact and income.

So here's my good news: there is a way forward, and in this book, I'll lay out the resources you need to succeed.

STUCK IN THE THORNY PATCH

If you're reading this book, you've likely gotten a dental practice, or two, or more, off the ground. You love the impact you have with your patients and feel ready to do more. You've topped out in your knowledge and need help to get to the next level.

You're finding it to be far thornier than imagined. This dentist-entrepreneur thing has become a real slog. Humbled, you can't figure out how to properly scale to achieve that passive income and ultimate impact you imagined. It feels like others have done it. Why can't you? What is the secret?

On the other hand, some of you have a good thing going but realize it could be better. Maybe much better. Why be an athlete if you can become an Olympic athlete? You want to shoot for the gold. You know that systems, processes, and culture are key, but how do you get those configured properly? You also likely understand that the best, thriving practices are being supported by a Dental Support Organization (DSO) structure. You might even realize you need this level of systems, structure, and support, but many dentists find the whole thing a bit mysterious. How does one get a DSO to work? And if you do, doesn't this mean giving up control? Social media seems abundant in opinions but lacking in real answers.

It is also lacking in answers on how to make progress; businesses can stall. Dentist-entrepreneurs find themselves working more than they ever thought they'd have to, and the business side is harder than expected. They're stretched so thin they can't imagine taking their businesses to the next level. Most move backward. In fact, they secretly know that even sticking to their current pace isn't sustainable. Is this you?

If so, you can feel a tipping point approaching. It's either find some strategies and tactics to save your entrepreneurial dreams or rethink your life path altogether.

THE PATH OUT OF THE THORNS

Many of you have come to the point my friend Chad reached, realizing that schooling represents only about 5 to 10 percent of what dentists do after graduation, especially if you want to scale your impact. As you've discovered, there's a lot more to running a dental business than standing chairside at the elbow of your patient.

So if you've only learned 5 to 10 percent of what you need to know, how do you fill in the 90 to 95 percent knowledge gap you have in order to scale successfully, especially given how stretched thin you already are?

First, you must realize that there's nothing about you that is the problem. You're not incompetent; you're not stupid. But you are missing something. If you've been suspecting that you are too inept to do it "right," it's time to recognize that your expectations have been one of the real blocks to progress.

You just haven't been taught that scaling up is actually really hard and takes time. Most people oversimplified it for you, and that didn't help. You need the truth.

It's a long journey with many legs, and each leg will present its own challenges. You don't have to pack for the entire journey all at once, but you do need to be able to look ahead to know what you ought to pack for the next leg. I'll open your eyes to what you'll face. As you reset your expectations, you can put your time and energy in the right places at the right times and maybe get some of that free time back.

Besides resetting your expectations about the challenges ahead, I'm going to help you meet them. This book is going to start demystifying the process of scaling up and moving into a DSO. Gaining clarity will be part of your solution toward growing a business that gets you that expanding dental empire with the passive income you want. It's not going to be quick or easy. You need tools and the right people to wield those tools. You'll need a support team and culture. And you'll need particular systems and processes geared toward your particular business in your special industry.

Knowing that you're undertaking a long journey that actually leads somewhere and understanding that along the way you'll take on tools and helpers to accompany and aid you on this entrepreneurial mission will change the way you think about what you actually want out of your business and how to go about getting it.

In short, you'll experience a paradigm shift. I've often told my wife how hard it is to have a paradigm shift. It means I will have to start believing something I don't believe today. But, by understanding what is possible and how to get it, you'll find a way to carve your path out of the thorns.

WHAT YOU'LL LEARN

This book is generally focused on helping you—the dentist—and your business team find success at each stage of business development in building a dental empire. It will show you how to create your own DSO or partner with a DSO to achieve your personal vision of success. Along the way, you'll learn the stages you should expect to face and what you'll experience during those stages. Each stage has its own lessons and mindsets you must take on in order to move through to the next milestone. Eventually, you'll get to the one that represents the scope of success you desire.

You generally can't leapfrog over these stages. Instead, you'll need to learn the fundamental practices and tools you need to have in place to achieve a strong base of operations as you move forward. These stages train you to become a clinical leader as well as a full-fledged business professional who knows how to keep a business in the dental industry healthy and thriving.

This book lays out the journey, helping you to understand the adventure you are taking into the unknown. You are going to discover new things that position you for practice expansion, and then entrepreneurial leadership, and then becoming an experienced executive—but above all that, you're going to discover things about yourself, strengths you can draw on to meet challenges, and the places where you need a team and support to keep your journey going forward. I've often said that entrepreneurship is more about personal development than it is about capitalism. Each of us "signs up" because we want to become something better. Patience, endurance, a willingness to learn and change—these are vital. If these are your strengths, get ready to start developing them. It's a beating you're going to have to enjoy.

HOW I CAME TO BE ON THIS JOURNEY WITH YOU

I graduated school with an accounting degree. I soon realized it wasn't a perfect fit. I worked as a financial planner, but I listened when my calling spoke and I started my entrepreneurial journey. It fed me! I started a consulting firm called Entrepreneur Advisors. Soon I had a radio show called *The Entrepreneur Life*. When my friend Chad called on my entrepreneurial consulting skills, I was delighted to help.

I soon found that healthcare is more complex than any other industry. The scope of the human component involved makes it especially challenging. It's one thing to have a bad product— say, clothes that customers find ill-fitting. It's another thing to have bad teeth or a bad heart or bad health as an outcome. There's an intensity to that.

And there's an intensity to the other human component: the practitioners themselves. Associates tend to want and need support as they navigate growing their businesses, but they sometimes don't accept it easily. They don't want to be told what to do, even as they want you to make sure they understand everything. In other words, I discovered that, unlike in any other industry, the "products" and the "producers" are all complex humans. The business goal is creating both happy patients and successful doctors and staff. This is the hardest business you will ever work in.

Meanwhile, I was realizing that the success Chad and I were having in transforming his business through a blend of entrepreneurship and healthcare wasn't something others in his situation were embracing. A lot of dentists perceived the type of help I offered—what amounted to a DSO, though I didn't realize it at the time—as part of a bad trend happening in the industry. I was hearing about these "terrible" DSOs, which dentists thought of as top-down private equity coming in and taking control. But that isn't what a DSO actually is—a DSO is for dentists looking for additional support to grow their business. Some perceived DSOs as swooping in to be controlling and aggressive. But the dentists themselves were creating and hiring DSOs, making for a sort of civil war within the industry.

I thought, *Man, a house divided is just going to split the industry, fall apart, and help no one.* And I had realized that this "warring" meant that, as a group, we weren't focusing on the right thing: creating a patient experience that could compete with the convenience and level of service being created in other industries. Instead, we were spending tons of dollars on legal battles with one another.

That's when I knew I needed to be transparent to the larger industry and see what I could do to help. I launched a podcast, *DSO Secrets,* for everybody looking for support and ideas to build the right DSO. And those who thought DSOs were evil could share, learn, and advise too. Together we could bring the industry together. The simple idea was to share those big, bad secrets and defuse all the wariness and anger dentist-entrepreneurs felt. I think we all benefited. Those who thought DSOs were evil (or not evil) could learn the inside scoop in secret without fear of judgment. Most found out that DSOs are simply a tool to be crafted in such a way that dentists receive maximum support. Those who do this will succeed. Those who don't will fail. The dentists are in a powerful position to win big.

The podcast—the number one podcast for DSOs—took off. In a transforming industry, lots of people had confusion and questions, so much so that we needed a *DSO Secrets* Facebook page where people could find support among like-minded people. They'd find resources and tools there too. But there was still a need for dentists even further down their entrepreneurial journey. At their stage, they needed access to coaches and specific learning through webinars and the like. This led to me sharing my expertise and, in 2020, becoming a partner in the Dentist Entrepreneur Organization. At DEO, dentist-entrepreneurs find ongoing learning, peer-to-peer networking, and direct coaching. Remember that you're on a long adventure. This book starts you off on the right foot. A journey of a thousand miles might start with a single step, but it sure helps if you have someone who also has access to the right shoes and a map!

WHAT THE BOOK *IS* AND *ISN'T*

This is a book sharing my experience and expertise, and the lessons I've learned helping dentists succeed in scaling up their businesses. Nothing you read should be construed as accounting or legal advice. You'll need to seek professionals in the compliance, accounting, and legal industries to keep you on the straight and narrow.

This book also won't provide cookie-cutter instructions, though it will give you the most detailed structure you will find in the marketplace. Every practice and every business can follow similar formulas despite the fact that each is unique in its own specific challenges. Some say that no two practices can be alike at the day-to-day level since they are planted in different soils and have different requirements—not just in terms of the setting, but also in terms of the people: the patients, the people working in your business, and especially you. And it's true that, in the end, you are going to design and build your dental empire according to the lay of your own land. But this book will give you the global map and a compass. After all, north is always going to be north. You no longer have to blindly wander in the wilderness.

Though I am going to take you through all the phases of building and growing, it would be impossible to answer every question specific to your situation and level of development. That
would be truly overwhelming, and reading it would be like,
um, pulling teeth. (Don't worry—I'll keep those puns to a mini-
mum.) If your questions are aching to be answered, you can
visit my podcast, poke through the *DSO Secrets* Facebook page,
or head over to DEO.

Note: In order to not bog down the book but still provide
you with multiple tools and video resources, I have set up
a website at DEOdentalgroup.com/dso-secrets/. You will
see a QR code on several chapters that will direct you
to these resources, which are constantly being updated
to stay contextually relevant and up to date on the latest
trends.

CHAPTER 1

Do You *Really* Want to Be a Dentist-Entrepreneur?

Do you? If you're ambitious, the answer seems obvious. You're thinking, *Yes! Absolutely! Hurry up and tell me how!*

Me too. I've always had an entrepreneurial spirit. At fourteen, I felt infuriated that children under fifteen couldn't hold formal jobs. A "silly government regulation" was crippling my ability to earn money for my essential teenage needs. Undeterred, I decided to start the greatest business any teenage entrepreneur could start in 1989: my very own lawn business. I partnered with my good friend Brian Fielding, and E&B Lawn Care was born.

I made my own flyers with the help of my dad, who worked in advertising. I traded some leftover pizza with the girl at a local printshop so she would make enough copies for the neighborhood. We used his four-door Chevy Corsica sedan like it was a Ford truck, hauling lawn mowing equipment to the nine homeowners we had convinced to let us do their dirty lawn work every week. I was killing it. And I was hooked.

After graduating from one of the top accounting schools in 2000, I got a "real job," but after one tax season, I knew it wasn't for me. I couldn't help but go back to my entrepreneurial ventures. I built a financial planning business and then created and hosted a radio show on entrepreneurship. I followed by opening my own consulting business.

Like many business owners, I put my blood, sweat, and tears into projects near and dear to my passion for success. My ambition ran free. And there was nothing wrong with that. Until there was.

One day, my wife, Michelle, walked in and told me, "I am headed to a counselor. Not sure I can handle all this. If you want to come, great. If not, at least I'm going to go."

I was ambitious but not an idiot. I told her I would go to counseling too.

At one of our first counseling sessions, I had an interaction that changed how I approached entrepreneurship and my life.

It started with the counselor saying, "Listen, Emmet, I'm much older than you and have seen this story again and again. Here's how the story ends based on how ambitious you are: you're going to be successful, and you're going to get a lot of accolades along the way. The road will be tough and will suck up most of your time, but the challenge combined with the accolades will only increase your motivation to want to be more ambitious."

Maybe she paused dramatically; I don't remember. But what she said next hit me like a ton of bricks: "I can tell you love your wife and children, so how does your four-year-old compete with all of this?"

"This" was me living out my entrepreneurial dreams, watching them come true, planting my flag on ever-increasing heights, and finding the grit and creativity and innovation that validated what I did and what I was.

The answer was obvious. Nothing could compete with *this*. What the world can give you for being ambitious is so big, so ego-boosting, so emotionally satisfying that even my cute, sweet, redheaded four-year-old could never compete with it. The shock of it.

The truth hit me at such a deep level that I couldn't go on as I had. I had to take control of my definition of success. How would I define who I wanted to be and why?

THERE'S A WRONG WAY TO DO IT

I'd been doing this entrepreneurship thing wrong. I'd made three major mistakes:

1. I hadn't figured out the full cost of the opportunity.

2. I hadn't defined my full and complete definition of success.

3. I hadn't prioritized my actions according to that definition.

You can see that these mistakes all worked together to compound the harm. Without considering *all* the costs of my entrepreneurial activities, I was failing to budget. It's not enough to think only in terms of money and hours put in. You expect those investments to pay you back. But divided attention or depleted energy while with your family, for instance—how do you get those back? How do you get back a memory you never made because you were at work?

Another problem to consider is what everyone else is sacrificing for your business. Clearly my wife had been sacrificing a lot or she wouldn't have made an appointment with a therapist. You don't have to make the same mistake. Make sure your most critical business partners are all aligned on what you'll achieve together.

Of course, entrepreneurs can't recognize the sacrificial pieces of a truly successful and happy life if they've never stopped to envision it. And without that model, how can you figure out where and how much you need to invest to find success in all the areas of your life? In my case, I was succeeding wildly in business, but I wasn't succeeding the same way and in the same magnitude in my family life. They were along for the ride—but it was my ride, not theirs.

I had to rebudget time, energy, and money for *all* the elements that would create a truly successful life for me and my family. Doing this can bring great anxiety. Most of you already realize that in business "bigger isn't better" if it means you have to cut into other precious elements of your life; but work is where you feel confident and safe, and changing that dynamic can be difficult. Yet what a relief to get life aligned and shed the guilt and worry over shortchanging life. It's a relief to realize that aligned and sometimes slower business growth lets you avoid bankrupting everything else.

FUEL YOUR DRIVE WITH AN ENTREPRENEURIAL WHY

Slowing or curtailing business growth doesn't change one hard reality: you still have a hard and taxing entrepreneurial journey ahead. A well-rounded life helps, but you'll still face crises as you feel your drive giving out. It's at those times that you need to rely on your Entrepreneurial Why. Your Entrepreneurial Why is the secret to your courage, persistence, and strength in the face of all manner of hardship.

Your Entrepreneurial Why (or Whys) is the thing you think of that never fails to kick in and move you forward. If you haven't figured out your Why, you need to do that now. You need it. Your Why drives you on when nothing else can.

It's not that I doubt your ambition, drive, and ability to work hard. If you're reading this book, you've self-screened and are clearly ambitious. But the hard work ahead is not as simple as you've been told, and it will take longer than you've been led to believe. This Brian Tracy quote sums it up: "There are no unrealistic expectations, only unrealistic time frames." In other words, be prepared for a long journey, recognizing that some high degree of sacrifice is required to hit your goals. The success has to be worth this sacrifice. Your Entrepreneurial Why supplies the reason it is.

There are as many Entrepreneurial Whys as there are dentists and entrepreneurs out there. The Why doesn't even have to be noble or deep to work. Did someone sneer and say you couldn't make your business work, and you get a fire in your belly every time you remember? That can drive you on. Did you have terrible teeth as a child and want to spare other children from having the same problem? If the thought inspires you, use it to press on.

The best Entrepreneurial Whys will help you when your strength is flagging and you want to throw in the towel. Actually write down your Whys. Read your list of reasons regularly to keep your ambition topped up. If you can then find ways to tie your Entrepreneurial Whys to your deepest purpose and values, to connect what you're doing to your sense of meaning and fulfillment, you'll be prepared to face any storms ahead.

RELATIONSHIPS

Relationships tend to fall by the wayside for most entrepreneurs. We don't make new friends, let alone keep up with old ones. First, acquaintances fall away. Then friends, followed by family members. Many of us fall into the trap of putting relationships on hold while we're busy.

But the lives of spouses, children, and friends keep going on even when our backs are turned. The successful entrepreneur can easily start to fall into a sense that all these relationships are transactional: I'm getting the family a house and the kids have extracurriculars, so I get to work. And I expect my spouse to attend to all the things that keep the household and family running. Of course, a sense of connection and intimacy fades. Or the lifestyle needs to keep improving to keep the transaction going, which makes the entrepreneurial work even more necessary. It's a vicious cycle.

Instead of a vicious cycle, create a virtuous cycle that keeps your relationships growing. Keep circling around to the relationships in your life to tend to them regularly. Your relationships will then nourish you and make you a better transformational leader in business while your business will support your family life and other important relationships.

You'll know you're succeeding when your most important relationships grow and thrive in parallel to your entrepreneurial activities. The virtuous cycle allows relationship activities and business to empower one another.

And consider this: you may not want to be a dentist or successful business executive forever. You want your life to come along with you to that day when you are no longer pouring your blood, sweat, and tears into your business. There's a lot of sacrifice; don't sacrifice your whole life in the bargain. Figure out how much you're willing to pay or sacrifice for the opportunity and why you're willing to do it. Getting straight with yourself gets you ready for a successful entrepreneurial journey.

We'll start the tactical part of the journey in the next chapter, when you will learn to become an ACE clinician, the set of capabilities behind every successful dentist-entrepreneur.

PERSONAL HOMEWORK TO COMPLETE

1. What does "real" success look like for me, right now and in the future?

2. What needs to happen for me, personally and professionally, to feel happy with my life over the next three years, five years, and ten years?

3. What relationships do I need to be the most careful in protecting if I pursue adding multiple locations?

4. What am I not willing to sacrifice to be a successful dental entrepreneur?

5. Why do I really want to build multiple locations?

6. What patient type am I most excited to serve?

7. What doctor associate type am I most interested in supporting and partnering with?

8. What is it about this challenge that I feel will be most rewarding personally?

9. Am I excited about moving from clinician to entrepreneur to executive and leading in a DSO? Why?

10. Am I excited to reduce my clinical time and devote myself to learning leadership skills?

11. Am I okay with doing all of this if the financial reward ends up not being as glorious as I dream it will be?

CHAPTER 2

The Clinician Behind All Your Future Success

ACE Clinician

It is easy to get overwhelmed and overfocused on all the business support and capabilities that need to be created to succeed, but the reality is that success in dentistry all starts with becoming a clinician, then recruiting and retaining successful clinicians to build a successful Dental Support Organization. Clinical excellence, clarity, and alignment have to be at the heart of your practice and your future growth. That means you've got to master being and teaching how to be a top-level clinician.

The core of being an ACE clinician is putting your patient-customers first—being a clinician who does the following:

- Is **available** to see patients when and where they need you

- Has the **capabilities** to serve and do the work the patient needs

- **Engages** effectively with patient-customers and with team members

In short, you need to become an ACE clinician to set the foundation for customer success that is worth scaling. Otherwise, you will become a conglomerate of practices with no real leadership on how to bring value to the marketplace. This is a trap that must be avoided to ensure long-term success.

This is vital to your future business plans because all scaling is accomplished through adding and effectively supporting associates. They are the product you are offering to the world via services. That means your clinical vision—your customer care—will always govern the business vision and business success.

AVAILABILITY

Imagine this: you've just left work and are racing to a birthday party for your child's best friend. You haven't picked up a gift yet because you had a last-minute project, which meant no lunch. Which means you're hungry too.

No worries—on your way, you can grab something from the toy store in the strip mall. And thank goodness for drive-throughs!

You stop at the toy store and discover they aren't open. You check your map app and find another store close by. You race there only to find the staff have cleaned up and are heading home. They seem to sneer as they look through the locked door.

If only someplace were *available*! Finding another store will mean no food for sure. You'll have to go into the mall. You'll be late to the party, and your child's present might not get there in time for the birthday boy's gift opening. You'll have to call and beg his mother to just hold off a bit. As you dial, you vow to never buy toys from the two closed toy stores again. What retailer nowadays closes so early?

We're not retailers, but availability still makes an enormous difference. Gone are the eighties and nineties, when dental offices were open only from ten o'clock to four o'clock three days a week. Nowadays, both parents work in most families, kids are in multiple after-school sports and activities, and it's harder to schedule visits. Patients mostly want to come in early in the morning or after four o'clock, when their kids are out of school and they are off work. Their retail mindset has bled over into their expectations of healthcare delivery. If Walmart is open for them 24/7, then healthcare professionals should offer more availability too. If Amazon is always available, why isn't dental appointment scheduling always on as well?

These days, availability is a career and business decision that means being there for your patients at the times they want and need. It is about investing in schedules and technology that make patient convenience your priority.

Imagine this: it's 6:30 p.m. and a patient shows up at the dental office of Dr. Smith. Dr. Smith has had a full day, with patients ranging from crying kids to seniors unhappy with the feel of their dentures. He's ready to go home. His staff is ready to go home. Dr. Smith has already cleaned up, changed out of his scrubs, and packed his belongings into his backpack. His staff has been closing down computers, filing paperwork, and ensuring everything is ready for the next day.

And now, just as they're about to lock the door, in walks the patient. Maybe this is a new patient with no appointment. Or the patient is just very late after being snarled in traffic. Or it's a patient who just broke a tooth and is in pain. Dr. Smith has a business decision to make. He puts his backpack down, ramps everything back up, and sees that patient.

His decision marks the beginning of his path to clinical mastery, and that path leads to increasingly better clinical results. Why?

First, think about what the patient will tell everyone about what the doctor was willing to do at closing time. Not just once, but every time dental work and dentists come up, in perpetuity. Can you hear the conversation? "Oh, you've got to see my guy. I showed up when he was turning off the lights, and he opened everything back up to take care of me. He really cares. I can't recommend him enough." This word of mouth, of course, increases patient flow. Dr. Smith has made the patient evangelical.

Second, because Dr. Smith showed his staff how serious he is about availability, they'll think differently about how the practice treats customers. That will change how they work and support patients, and they will begin scheduling based on patient needs. Again, patient flow increases.

Dr. Smith's availability mindset isn't just about patients who show up late or those with emergencies. His availability mindset also impacts his desire to be open on weekends or mornings or to complete same-day treatment. Dr. Smith sees more patients than a doctor unwilling to be more available. And this snowball effect of availability changes Dr. Smith's clinical capability.

Improved patient availability along with word of mouth from patients who know a dentist that schedules according to their needs means Dr. Smith is seeing a volume that other dentists aren't seeing. It's a trickle at first, but the flow keeps increasing.

Availability is something any dentist can do, no matter their schooling or clinical capability. Availability means Dr. Smith will see more reps in his career than other dentists. He will simply have more experience than other dentists with fewer patients and less volume. This is why availability is the foundation for clinical mastery of becoming ACE.

The best part about availability is that it is a mindset. It only requires us to be more willing and open to catering to patients' hours and needs. You don't need a new skill to earn the A in ACE, simply a more patient-centered mindset.

CAPABILITY

Let's imagine a capability scenario. A patient meets with Dr. Sam for a procedure Dr. Sam may not have done often or is not comfortable with. It's also not a procedure he loves to do, so he refers the patient to another doctor with a better skillset in this area. He tells the patient, "This isn't a procedure we see very often. Let me refer you to someone who does."

Dr. Sam believes he's done right by the patient. It's better, he thinks, for the patient to have a willing and able clinician. Unfortunately, the patient isn't feeling well taken care of the way Dr. Sam might expect.

Customer feedback shows that a referred patient has one mindset: *My dentist can't do what's necessary to solve my problem.* If that patient is in pain, they will take it one step further and think, *My doctor doesn't know how to relieve my pain.* The patient will then tell others what happened, something along these lines: "I really love my dentist, but he can't really do procedures if you're in pain or need something complicated done." The patient has lost confidence in Dr. Sam's *capabilities.*

Customers go where they find the most value, and they define value based on how they felt during the appointment. If you want to succeed with patients, they should get your empathy, skills, and experience to best serve them and their needs. To provide the best care, you make decisions when it comes to your time and expertise. But most patients don't want to be ping-ponged from one dental practice to another. It's more scheduling they have to do in busy lives. They want you to be available and come with the capability to provide their care.

That makes expanding your capability to do more for your patients critical to becoming a master clinician. By combining expanding capability with availability, you're building incredible value for your patients. And the best news is that most dentists are unwilling to do this, which means you're sharpening your competitive edge as well. So be willing to stretch yourself while also knowing your limits.

Expanding the capability in your practice to perform more and more procedure types will naturally move you farther down the road to master clinician. What's best for patients is getting their work done timely and effectively. You must meet their needs with capabilities.

ENGAGEMENT

As intent as patients are in their hunt for availability and capability, they also want a level of personalization. They want the sense of a best-case scenario experience. You've probably heard the term *emotional intelligence* (EQ). We call it engagement, and it levels up our clinician mastery.

Patients are experts in only one thing: how they feel. They don't understand clinical care from a perspective of margins or treatment modalities. They simply interpret everything around them by how convenient and friendly and comfortable they felt the practice was.

Engagement is about connecting and leading patients. I follow three rules:

Rule 1:
Beware of Clinical Speech, Education, or Questioning

Doctors sometimes forget they're doctors and start conversations using jargon. No one likes to have a conversation that requires a translator. Using jargon can also make the dentist appear to be purposely speaking this way to reinforce their authority-figure status, which can make patients feel patronized. Patients who feel patronized will feel defensive. When a doctor uses jargon, or a clinical tone, instruction or education may come across as judgment or a shaming. Using a clinical tone in questioning can come across the same way.

Let's take Dr. Sheila: she has just begun her dental career and is excited to have her first patient. It happens to be a seven-year-old girl and her mother. The young patient has a lot of issues and decay. Dr. Sheila asks her a simple clinical question: "How often do you brush your teeth?"

Mom frowns and says defensively, "I remind her every night." She feels embarrassed, shamed, and judged. She's already decided she doesn't like this doctor or how she feels.

Dr. Sheila is taken aback. How did smooth sailing turn into choppy waters?

Well, the seas started to get choppy with that first seemingly simple clinical question to the daughter, which Mom heard as "Do you have a good mother who takes care of you, or do I need to call CPS for negligent childcare?" Faced with an authority figure in a white lab coat, adults sometimes hear and fear the worst.

The lesson is that no matter how unfair you may think it is, clinicians must realize that everything they say is going to be considered in the context of judgment and shaming. To improve engagement, remember that people feel intimidated or nervous when they visit, so put yourself in their shoes and approach diagnostic questioning with empathy.

To follow Rule 1, remember that though the object of conversations may be dental health and treatment, the subject is your patients' confidence and connection to you.

Rule 2: Lower Shame and Guilt

Here's an example of a pediatric script that works really well for the Dr. Sheila scenario:

"Can I tell you something? I am so grateful you came in today. You don't know how many people don't bring their children in to get seen. You'd be surprised how many people just skip their appointments and don't take care of their oral health."

And to the patient: "Now, I see lots of opportunities to improve your health and your smile. And here's the good news—there's nothing here I can't fix." Dr. Sheila smiles.

Mom feels supportive of Dr. Sheila's efforts to help her daughter. She's ready to help improve her daughter's oral health. And the daughter doesn't feel scolded or scared.

Dr. Sheila performs the procedures, and a team member who also has good engagement provides education and instruction for home care. As the mother and daughter schedule their next appointment, the team member provides a take-home worksheet that they can refer to and use to track their efforts. It's a gentle reminder offered in a nonthreatening manner in a safe environment. The same script and approach, with some adjustments, can work for any age.

Lowering shame and guilt for patients fulfills Rule 2. Remember that patients are only experts on how they feel.

Rule 3: Build Value

A popular entrepreneurial quote says, "Price is an issue when value is not apparent." You'll build value for your patients when you build clarity for them on the impact of taking or not taking action on your recommendations. Each patient is asking themselves the same question: *If I don't spend the money and time here, where is a better place for me to spend it?* Most dentists and teams have not been taught how to create value—how to compete against Amazon, Target, and every TV or social media ad bombarding their patients. The answer boils down to a few basic principles:

1. Identify the problem that would be meaningful for the patient to solve. Do they like sharing bacteria with their family, or is that something that would be meaningful for them to reduce? Do they have an event that they would like to look better for? Is there a relationship that they are hoping to advance? How is what you are about to recommend going to impact any of these opportunities or challenges?

2. Give a confident solution. People follow confidence. Many clinicians are so focused on education and providing choices that they forget the customer wants leadership and direction. Yes, they want it delivered in an empathetic way, but they want clarity on how to achieve the best outcome for them.

For instance:

> *"Listen, you have some cavities, which means you've got some live bacteria that is growing in your mouth. This concerns me because you're swallowing it every day, which lets it affect your growth, your health, and your well-being. It's also contagious. So, when you share a drink or a fork or spoon, you're passing it on to others in your family. I'd like to remove and eliminate it from your mouth."*

Notice how you're avoiding jargon and building value by clarifying action versus nonaction? You continue on:

> *"So here's what I want to do today. I want to remove all that bacteria. I want to free up your body's ability to fight other infections you might have going on and not waste your body's time and energy. Plus, I'll be leaving you looking healthier, with clean teeth, better breath, and more confidence in your smile."*

Compare that to "So, are you brushing your teeth? It looks like you've got some caries on your anterior..." or "I am going to do some fillings, if you want, or we can do a crown; it's really up to you on what you feel like doing. There are lots of ways we can approach this." These statements build no value for your patients and destroy confidence.

Build value by clearly defining what action and nonaction outcomes look like and giving clear direction. This follows Rule 3.

ACE

When you're available, capable, and engaged, you'll be able to build the clinical value you provide into what's most important to the patient. That will encourage them to come into your office and pay for your services. It means you will see more patients, treat more patients, and expand your brand in the marketplace. It will build loyalty and make a greater impact on the health of your community.

Becoming an ACE clinician takes a mindset of willingness: the willingness to be available, to learn the new things that make you more capable, and to engage in patient interactions with empathy, understanding, and clear communication. By making ACE a habit in your practice and training your associates to do the same, you'll become ready to take your business to the next level.

It's constructive to think about ACE clinical mastery as a phase in your business development. Spend time here instead of rushing to the next leg of your journey. Ensuring that you and all your current associates are actively and routinely focused on availability, capability, and engagement is the best and first step toward your future and ever-increasing success.

After everyone's ACE-ing it, you'll be ready for the next phase, which you'll be learning about in the next chapter.

CHAPTER 3

The Entrepreneur

Becoming an Expert in Multiple Industries

Many ACE clinicians aspire to entrepreneurship. Most books are written as if it's the ultimate stage of business success. I aspired to it too. My problem was that, in the beginning, I was terrible at being an entrepreneur and I didn't see it for what it was.

Like many of you, my fire for the entrepreneurial journey drove me forward. Continuing on can be a grueling slog, but the first attribute of any entrepreneur is to put one foot in front of the other, believing each step is a step closer to a better future. We ferociously learn everything we can about business. We work to be the smartest person we can to take on this next vision for growth. We become the smartest person in the room.

Unfortunately, the transition to entrepreneur leaves a lot of us slogging around in circles. As entrepreneurs, we're the hub of the business; everything revolves around us. Meanwhile, we're learning how to create an actual business with some (or maybe many) gaps in our systems and organization. We try to fill in the holes on the go, but a lot of us feel too stretched to actually find more permanent solutions. We're stuck and overworked, with no clear path out of this morass of over-work and overwhelm. I've seen many dentist-entrepreneurs in this situation start to burn out.

It's hard to make the leap from being primarily a clinician at chairside to being primarily an entrepreneur. The key to doing so without burning out is a change in mindset: knowing what to focus on and which fires to "let burn."

CLINICIAN-TO-ENTREPRENEUR WARNINGS

It's important to make a distinction between being an ACE clinician, which most books will call "the technician," and being an entrepreneur. In the beginning of the entrepreneurial journey, most of us tend to make the same general mistake: we keep being primarily a technician who is also an entrepreneur instead of an entrepreneur who is also a technician. In fact, we don't even put a lot of thought into what being an entrepreneur is. That is, what sort of things does an entrepreneur do, no matter what the industry? What are the traits of entrepreneur-ship that drive success? Instead we view entrepreneurship as simply an expansion of our technical skills.

Here is your warning:

Without that examination, it's easy to over-rely on your technical grounding. It's your expertise and you're comfortable there. You can see the symptoms of this in the intense level of detail most technician-based entrepreneurs get stuck in. They treat everything as the most important item.

A seasoned entrepreneur, though, recognizes that technical expertise is now just a *context* for their business. The business itself is the opportunity to have greater impact. And that can be uncomfortable for many, especially when they have paid so much for their technical degree. But not making the transition gets uncomfortable too. Continuing to think like a technical expert usually means remaining a beginner entrepreneur who doesn't grow quickly enough to meet the challenges of business ownership. That's when the entrepreneurial journey begins feeling like a grim slog.

The following are some symptoms of this:

- Feeling behind at all times

- An increasing sense of losing control

- Constant feeling of anxiety and stress

- Inability to prioritize ideas about the business

- Not enough hours in the day

- Hypervigilance and fear that something important isn't being attended to

- Not knowing how to fix things so that they will run smoothly

- Feeling like you're failing or beaten

Two pieces of good news. First, these are symptoms of beginning entrepreneurship. You're just stuck in technician mode. Second, you can outgrow this and begin to enjoy being an entrepreneur after all.

THE POWER OF ENTREPRENEURSHIP

Not that it's going to be easy, of course, but it's amazing how a sense of progress, growth, and renewed excitement can make hardship worthwhile.

I love the growth of being an entrepreneur. Entrepreneurs find fortitude by bringing out strengths and abilities they often didn't even know they had. That personal development brings self-respect and confidence. There's nothing like overcoming a challenge to make you feel like a winner!

As entrepreneurs, we learn to be creative, inventive, resourceful innovators, improving some piece of the world. We get to be fired up, indulging our passion for learning. We are discoverers who find revelations in both success and failure. Self-motivated ambition spurs our actions. Every day is new, not lived on autopilot. What a job description! Sure, it can be hard, but on those days, we can lean into our Why to transcend challenges.

I've found that these are the top three skills a clinician needs when first transitioning to entrepreneur:

1. **The math:** Make financial calculations as you leave the chair. How much time can you work on the business instead of working in the business? Get help here from a spreadsheet guru to help build out your assumptions and do the math accurately. Know what adding an associate will do to the dental practice financials, what patient flow is needed, and what capabilities the associate will need to have to make it all work.

2. **The learning:** Realize that deep and ferocious learning is part of the job. I hope you're hungry for some humble pie. To run your business, you're going to need

to learn information across several disciplines beyond clinical—HR, marketing, accounting, compliance, IT—disciplines that others have earned degrees in. And you can't take your time about it. You don't have to become an expert on all of it. But you need at least a grounding in order to talk to experts and ask questions.

3. The decisiveness: Decide what role or roles you'll invest the most time in as the owner-entrepreneur. Division of labor starts with you. A clear understanding of your strengths and weaknesses as an entrepreneur is critical to growing the business. It's time to stop being the smartest one in the room. Who are you going to delegate to and what are you going to expect them to do? As you learn about all the different areas your business relies on, you'll know those you are best at and where you need help. You'll need to hire others to fill the roles you won't be shouldering. Back to doing the math as you grow.

Addressing these three challenges goes a long way in officially behaving as an entrepreneur. You've made room for entrepreneurial activities away from the chair, you've learned enough to understand the range of business activities you need performed, and you've figured out which part of those you'll take on yourself. In parallel, you'll be working on a greater challenge: developing yourself.

THE ULTIMATE SRP: SELF-AWARENESS, RISK TOLERANCE, AND POSITIONING

Nothing reveals your true self like taking on the unknown. As I tried to move from entrepreneur to successful entrepreneur, I realized I needed to cultivate three areas: self-awareness, risk tolerance, and positioning.

First, I came to understand that **self-awareness** was the key to continual growth. Without self-awareness, how, for instance, would I know what direction my personal growth should take?

Second, I had to rethink my understanding of **risk tolerance**. Risk, I learned, is not only about taking leaps. It's also about loosening control. Finally, I had to learn to **position** myself as a leader. There is now a bigger mission and a bigger picture than your technical niche. You're not just in charge of the trees; you're in charge of the forest.

S – Self-Awareness

As a new entrepreneur, I had the sense to realize I didn't know what I was doing. Solution? Learning! I dove in. I read 130 books on business, marketing, and finance. I spent thousands of dollars on coaches, consultants, and conferences. One year, I spent over $50,000 on coaching platforms.

But I was still falling short as an entrepreneur. Why?

Eventually, through my particular entrepreneurial path, I began to see that my problem was that no matter what I learned, I couldn't scale much past myself. This was the beginning of my self-awareness.

It didn't matter if I was the smartest one in the room, the one who had read over a hundred books. It didn't matter if I had made myself the best technician. It didn't matter if I could be a rugged individualist, able to perform every function in my business. In order to scale, I needed others, and I needed the systems and processes to support them.

I needed to support them. What did I need to develop in myself that would serve my team? What were the systems and processes that would help a team do their best for clients? I'd finally realized what I was missing: the leadership piece that leans on self-awareness.

The leadership breakthrough comes when an entrepreneur begins purposely developing the character and personality traits that help them invest in others' abilities. Demonstrating humility, releasing ego, understanding that they can't do it alone, that they *need* the help of their team—self-awareness makes entrepreneurs into leaders.

When that clicked for me, I went from being a lone entrepreneur to running a $100 million plus company.

R – Risk Tolerance

Most people think of risk tolerance in the context of investment, say in the stock market or Bitcoin. Surprisingly, I've found that very few dentists have issues with these kinds of investments. They involve a mathematical assessment the dentists feel comfortable doing or, like many others, the dentists simply follow the crowd.

But how comfortable are you with handing over things to your team members or trusting a partner? Few things bother entrepreneurs as much as giving up control. Giving up control can feel like jumping out of an airplane. Without a chute. But loosening your grip is a necessary risky step in becoming a great entrepreneur.

This will feel different than risking money. Giving up control over your business, your baby, this grand creation you made from your blood, sweat, and tears—well, that's personal. Your business has become part of your identity, infused with your dreams and your ego. If it fails or does poorly, that reflects on who you are. It's not just your life now; it's your future too.

It will also feel different from the risk you took in moving from clinician to beginning entrepreneur. Making that move had some comfort built in. You were still making all the decisions: the marketing decisions, the IT decisions, the paid time off decision, the HR hiring—all of them. You felt in control, even though you'd taken the big step of business ownership.

But all entrepreneurs hit a human threshold: you can't be the only one reacting to opportunities and threats. I've seen a lot of entrepreneurs try, holding on to the reins with white-knuckled hands. The fear of handing control to others who might end up doing something wrong wins out over the common sense of delegating.

The truth is that others *will* do things wrong. The consequences will cost something. But that only means you need to invest in your people. They need space to learn and mentoring to grow.

You will do things wrong too. You're going to have the wrong people in the wrong places. You're going to have some turnover. This is just entrepreneurship as it matures. It's a learning process that doesn't end in perfection, only improvement. This is the really hard part—executing on your vision *through other people.* It's a risk and it's painful, trusting others and watching them screw up. Think of it as a growing pain as you get better at being in charge.

Acclimating to being in charge of others who then take control over aspects of your business will require patience and tolerance and the acknowledgment that sometimes there is more than one right way to do something.

P – Positioning

A lot of entrepreneurs have a typical organizational chart in their head, the old inverted pyramid that puts the boss on top and tiers of management and employees below. But that's not actually how roles work in the entrepreneur's day-to-day practice. You're at the center of things, connected to everyone, the hub of the wheel. You're the first expert on product and service, and the one everyone comes to for final say. That won't work in a scaled-up business. Its domain is just too sprawling for one person to manage everything.

As your business matures, you'll need to start transitioning away from being at the center. Let others become decision makers and problem solvers. This is a process, of course, which means you have to concentrate on making it happen until it becomes comfortable.

For instance, if you have a marketer and something is going wrong in marketing, there are two ways to solve it. You can tell your marketer to get out of the way so you can do it, or you can position yourself as a coach, teaching them what to do.

It's important to start learning how to behave as a leader who develops people. This is how you scale, creating a talent pool to deploy. The entrepreneur who constantly deploys themselves will be doing chores all day long—not the best use of your time and abilities.

Your direct involvement in daily work falls on a spectrum from "Yes, this is something only I can or should do" to "Anyone can do this. Delegate." Repositioning yourself means asking yourself, *Can I take a step back from this task or project?* During this phase of your journey toward your DSO dreams, you're still going to have to be a technician and entrepreneur on some things. You're still developing the team. But, meanwhile, keep repositioning yourself to back away from the things best delegated to others.

Fear will try to play head games with you, worrying you with thoughts of impending disaster or tempting you to follow behind your team as they tackle tasks. Resist. Double down on developing your people and teams. Help others become ACE clinicians and self-managers and decision makers. In a way, you're making yourself obsolete, thus moving yourself to higher and higher levels of value creation. Creating a successful business isn't about you, a brilliant entrepreneur, at the center as much as it is about transitioning to a team environment as quickly as possible and you continuing to move up in your leadership and development.

ENTREPRENEURIAL CEILINGS

When I was a terrible entrepreneur who thought that "just a little more knowledge" was my ticket to success, I quickly found out that learning "enough" meant trying to drink from an information firehose. I was reading across so many industries. I never knew enough.

And I couldn't imagine where the learning curve flattened.

That's a common feeling for dentist-entrepreneurs, one born of a classic mistake: getting stuck in too many details because *the entrepreneur is trying to run their business like a technician.*

Part of the problem is that being an entrepreneur is a transitional phase. A phase of learning and character development.

The entrepreneurial phase gives you the chance to take an off-ramp. Do you really want to put in the work of growing into a DSO? You've weathered a lot to get this far. It's been an adventure, full of discovery and the self-respect that comes from taking on challenges and risks. But scaling up has still more challenges in store. The most difficult leg of your journey comes next as you pass through a phase I call the Dark Tunnel.

CHAPTER 4

The Dark Tunnel

Just When You Thought It Would Get Better

Maturing as an entrepreneur, a dentist–business owner starts feeling pretty good, pretty confident, pretty bona fide. "I've got this!" After all, you're chugging away on that unicycle. You're juggling with such expertise that you could join the circus. In fact, before you became so good at your business, it did kind of feel like a circus. But you've got the hang of it now, and you've advanced steadily, juggling three, four, and now five balls.

Your entrepreneurial journey has been tiring, but you know it will be smoothing out soon. You can feel it. Somewhere ahead are beautiful days at your beautiful entrepreneurial destination. It could be just around the next curve. The next practice you buy. Excited and ready to arrive, you decide it's time to up your game. No more putting it off. It's time to start swapping out balls for chainsaws. It's the big leagues now.

But around the next curve isn't your destination. It's a tunnel. A Dark Tunnel.

THE DARK TUNNEL

The Dark Tunnel is a rite of passage that, unfortunately, no entrepreneur can avoid if they want to grow beyond a handful of offices. It's a mostly unexpected leg of the journey, and it's hard—hard enough to set you back on your heels and make you feel you're about to lose everything.

It takes entrepreneurs by surprise because successfully juggling three to five offices makes them think that one more will be more or less the same game. But that one more scale-up attempt suddenly exceeds juggling capacity. The stress is the kind that can make your hair go gray and then fall out. It's clearly not more of the same. It's a totally different game.

Doing my *DSO Secrets* podcast, over and over I have heard from dentist-entrepreneurs blindsided by this traumatic phase of their business journey. They don't know what is happening or, crucially, why this is happening. At the root of this confusion is a lack of scaling experience. There's only so much an entrepreneur can juggle without specific solutions—it's a simple matter of capacity.

THE THREE C's OF THE DARK TUNNEL

The Dark Tunnel can feel life-threatening, complete with the flight, fight, or freeze trigger. You will feel overwhelmed. No matter how perfectly you execute on your business growth, you will hit this phase. Besides feeling overwhelmed, you will suffer the three Cs:

- Increasing **costs**. At certain points in scaling, the required resources cause costs to rise steeply. For instance, there's no off-the-shelf products for strategically growing your practice, so you'll need a strategic and project management team to make anything happen. You'll find leadership is not cheap but is necessary if you're going to scale and grow. During these periods, profits will get very lean. You'll remember days with fewer practices and more money. This phase of growth and little income can last a long time.

- A loss of **confidence**. As costs mount and you feel increasingly overwhelmed, you'll have a sense of going backward. Things won't be getting easier. You promised yourself and maybe others that just around the corner were easier days and more profitability. You were wrong and you'll be scrambling to figure out why. Moving backward into beginner status is naturally a blow to your confidence. You'll start to wonder if you're not the businessperson you thought yourself to be.

- Increasing **complexity**. If you have children, do you remember the difference in impending chaos when you went from one child to two? How about from two to three? Imagine eight or ten—your ballooning number of offices will become increasingly complex operations in terms of systems and coordination and management. You have a lot of humans to manage in a healthcare environment with very few resources easily available—the ultimate complexity of entrepreneurship.

THE BUSINESS OF DENTAL HEALTHCARE: A CHANGING, COMPLEX INDUSTRY

Dentists scaling up their businesses will do so in a complicated, shifting setting. Understanding why is key to finding the right coping strategies—the best solutions—to safely come out on the other side of the Dark Tunnel.

Why is a scaled dental business so complex? It comes down to two factors:

Complexity 1: The 100 Percent Human Factor

If we classify all businesses according to human involvement, we end up with only two categories. The first category is the industry that manufactures a product. In that industry, humans may manage, and they may even create, but the product is an object, a nonhuman. An artist, for instance, is a human that creates an object of art. In an auto factory, humans manage humans who oversee robotic assembly lines that manufacture a vehicular product.

And then there's the second category, the 100 percent human category. If we agree that a human being is a most complex and mysterious creature, so complicated that many whole branches of learning are dedicated to it—*us*—we begin to get an inkling of how much complication can get baked into a business in which input and output are both human.

That's where you are: every dental business falls into the 100 percent human category. Not only are management and employees human—*the product is human too*. And that product is your patient.

Humans need a lot of direction. They need a lot of validation. They need to be paid on time, to be trained properly, and for their computers to work. Overload is bound to happen as you open more offices.

Complexity 2: The Healthcare Industry
Is Under Development

The second complexity is that we're in a consolidating indus-try. Not consolidated. Consolidating, as in, we're still working out the kinks. What do I mean?

It means no matter how excited someone is about scaling the dental industry, the dental industry doesn't have the tools to scale. The customer technology, the IT support, the bank-ing infrastructures, the HR software—none of that has been figured out or standardized. Just ask anyone responsible for doing credentialing or verifying claims for a patient and you'll see what little standardization exists. Though dentists and business owners are excited to do multilocation sites, the enterprise solutions and vertical links that would simplify complexity have yet to be created.

Contrast that with other industries that are already consol-idated—fast-food chains, for instance. They're not trying to figure out how to get all their stores' data up to corporate. That solution has already been built. If I wanted to get into the fran-chise business and scale up a host of fast-food places, I'd have many companies and choices that could provide me support.

I often share the analogy that dentistry is like this beauti-ful piece of land we have all been given. We can build a shop-ping center or homes or apartments on this beautiful piece of land, and it would bring great value to the community and to investors who wanted to support; however, there is no Home Depot and no contractors. So most of us in the early stages find ourselves chopping wood and making nails.

THREE STEPS TO SAFELY NAVIGATE THE TUNNEL

Step 1: Revisit Your Why

In Chapter 1, you found your Entrepreneurial Why, that reason that never fails to drive you forward when the going gets tough. Since your Why drives you on when nothing else can, you'll need it during a time of crisis, which the Dark Tunnel certainly is.

However, if you discover that your Why doesn't inspire you as much as it did before, this may be a sign that you don't really have the appetite to grow larger. And there's no reason you need to. You've worked hard to become a successful entrepreneur. If you're in the groove of that, you enjoy your work, you have a comfortable lifestyle, and you feel fulfilled, remaining where you are or becoming smaller may be a better choice than growing further.

Something similar is depicted in TV shows and movies where someone becomes a victim of their own success, promoted to a desk job when they really only thrived out in the field, making discoveries or piloting ships or mentoring others. Growth of locations is not everyone's be-all and end-all. Going forward is a lot of work if you're not going to feel happy in the end.

I'd like those of you who are still determined to continue into the tunnel to consider whether or not you have the stamina and resources to persevere through this daunting phase. Think about not only your sacrifices but also those of your family. Because the Dark Tunnel is so taxing, it's important to make sure to recommit and get buy-in.

Step 2: Embrace Your Humility and Get Help

Surviving the Dark Tunnel will first and foremost take humility. Scaling up will, at some point, force you to take on new ways of doing things. You'll have to learn a lot around delegation and how to financially do it quickly and effectively.

Even so, humility will inform you that you can no longer avoid getting professional help and advice to compensate for your own weaknesses and knowledge gaps. You must start hiring an executive team, experts to help you navigate uncertain times. I'll talk through resources for executive support in later chapters.

Step 3: Join an Organization or Partnership

You don't have to travel through the Dark Tunnel alone. The whole reason Dental Support Organizations began to form was to support the unique problems clinicians have. Besides hiring your own executive team members as you move through this transitional phase, you can join the Dentist Entrepreneur Organization (DEO) to get peer support and expert advice. DEO programs help dental groups in a variety of growth stages.

Another option is to partner with someone who has already emerged from the tunnel. Their maturity and experience can help some dental groups leapfrog the Dark Tunnel state.

An example of this is the DSO I created with Chad, Community Dental Partners (CDP). CDP is built specifically to solve for the Dark Tunnel. We allow dentists and entrepreneurs entering the Dark Tunnel to choose any services they need help with, for instance, activity around financial support, marketing, HR, compliance, and IT. By partnering with CDP, dentists and their business partners can continue to build their vision but are given a huge tool belt of resources they currently don't have.

Whatever path you choose, my goal is to help entrepreneurs get through this Dark Tunnel and move on to having a bigger impact in healthcare. But because they hit the Dark Tunnel, with the increased costs, the loss of confidence, and the confounding complexity, these entrepreneurs often end up stymied and stifled.

The Dark Tunnel is long, but there is a light at the end. Once you get out into the light, you'll discover something wonderful. If you've learned to be an executive, if you're doing it right, it all gets easier. We'll talk about that in the next chapter.

CHAPTER 5

The Pinnacle of Impact

Executive Leadership

A s an ACE clinician riding the unicycle, everything was about you. When you became a juggling entrepreneur, everything still revolved around you, including a team or sets of teams who relied on you. Moving through the Dark Tunnel forces you to get the right talent in the right roles because at some growth point, no one can keep juggling it all.

Congratulations on doing what you needed to do to finally come out of the worst leg of your entrepreneurial journey. The Dark Tunnel is useful for more than just rapidly putting together a big-impact team. It's useful to prove to you that you can no longer be an entrepreneur as you knew it. Yes, you'll take that entrepreneurial energy forward—in fact, it'll be your secret sauce as you find creative, innovative solutions in your business—but from now on you will be an executive.

This might understandably make you nervous. After all, you didn't go to school for that. But you'll learn along the way as you have with everything else. And great news—if you're doing it right as an executive, every step gets a little easier as you scale. Or maybe your pain tolerance is just higher.

FROM ENTREPRENEUR TO EXECUTIVE

When I had my consultant business, I was called in to assist a construction company. While the entrepreneurial owners were doing well and making money, they had a problem to solve: "We have no time," they told me. Their phones hadn't stopped ringing since I'd come in the door.

Their business had grown, but, as with so many entrepreneurs, the owners still had a tight hold on things. They were convinced they were the only ones who could do the jobs that needed to be done and so had backed themselves into a time-crunch corner. However, the one resource you can't make more of, even as a successful entrepreneur, is time. They were in their own Dark Tunnel.

Their first step was to start reinvesting some of their profit to build out an executive team. We trained the business owner on things like how to use a CFO (chief financial officer), how to use a COO (chief operating officer), how to hire a marketing director, and how to create a meeting and communication cadence to lead their new executive team.

Eventually, the owners moved from doing a lot of tasks they had once done on their own to accepting and reviewing reports from their team. With a couple of meetings a week, they regularly received a full review of what was happening in their business.

I checked in at the eighteen-month mark. The revenue had ballooned. "How do you feel it's going?" I asked, knowing they were happy with the growth.

"Well, my revenue is up five times what it was. But this," he said, picking up his silent cell phone, "has been the real success."

Besides growing his business, my client now had a strong team to back him as his business grew and scaled, so he had gotten back his greatest resource: time.

So what does it mean to be an executive? It's stepping back from your technician and business-owner mindset and moving into a new level of mindset altogether.

YOUR NEW ROLE: STRATEGIC VISIONARY

Back in Chapter 2, you did some looking ahead, envisioning what you wanted for your life and your business. This imagining may have felt like dreaming at the time, but now that you are here, this ability to envision the future is crucial to the success of your business. You now lead a team of executives and employees. Where are you leading them? What does it look like? What are the rewards that everyone the business touches will reap? What do you see when you look far into the distance through your telescope?

And though there might be one obvious sight your telescope shows you—say Mars—your telescope will continue to provide you a lot of other sights too. You will see the Moon, its craters, and asteroids—as a visionary, you're going to have a lot to occupy your attention. Can you clearly communicate it?

If you see your far-off vision clearly, you'll be able to answer these questions:

- Who are we being heroes to?

- How do we want to serve them?

- What changes do we want to make in their lives?

- How do we want to behave as a team to make this happen?

In essence, you'll start creating a clear business mantra and culture for the company. A business's mantra is a short and memorable phrase that informs your company's way of thinking or acting. As such, it serves as a North Star that can point your people in the same direction, the right direction. For more information on building a mantra, I would suggest Patrick Lencioni's book *The Advantage*.

TRIANGULATE USING SPC

A mantra also provides a backbone for strategic planning, project management, and communication cadences. Strategic planning, the projects that make those plans a reality, and the communication that keeps everything greased are the three overarching business functions that you, as an executive, must oversee as a strategic visionary. You'll oversee the people directly in charge of them to make sure your company is always heading toward what you see in your telescope.

This is more important than it might seem at first. Imagine charting a course from one continent to another, with specific departure and arrival coordinates. An error of just a fraction of a degree would take your ship wildly off course. Strategic planning, project management, and communication cadences—SPC—are triangulation tools that keep you on course.

Strategic Planning

Strategic planning flows directly from your vision. If you look through the telescope toward the day that you have revolutionized healthcare, in the not-too-far-off future you may need to start acquiring certain locations or businesses, invest in research and development, improve systems and processes, start recruiting and developing certain talent, and so on. Focusing on these doesn't require a telescope so much as the shorter sight of binoculars. It's your job to communicate what you've seen and supply binoculars to those who must focus on the strategies that will achieve your vision. Meet your project management team.

Project Management

A company only has so many resources to spend. Someone must decide, from among all the choices your vision provides, which can and should be pursued, according to return on investment. This team sits between your C-suite and the managers, directors, and team heads who must execute. The project management team is like a secret row on the typical organizational chart, taking whiteboard ideas and breaking them down for the managers, directors, and their teams. They also buffer managers from unfiltered ideas and wish lists that might otherwise scatter their efforts. Our project managers work off a simple acronym we call DOPE:

- Document all ideas and potential strategic initiatives.

- Organize these ideas to better understand scope, time-lines, and responsibilities.

- Prioritize these ideas based on return on investment and resource allocation.

- Execute on these ideas by utilizing project management principles.

Remember that it continues to be your job to build out your team, including these project managers, to give them the support they need. People come to me all the time about the project management team we have. They note that we go beyond the manager and the director, adding people doing project management. No one else does that, they'll note. But this secret row on the organizational chart is the reason your business can grow and scale so quickly.

Communication

Though the Dark Tunnel should have taught you the necessity of delegating, one area you'll stay active in is communication. Without it, no one in your business can lead, organize, coordinate, influence, or teach. Clear and regular communication flows down from you and up to you. How else can you properly influence outcomes?

How much and how often should you communicate? Too much communication ends in micromanagement and can come across as critical. Too little communication ends in disconnect and leadership gaps. Striking a balance is crucial. This is your communication cadence—how often you'll review your team's feedback and keep pushing your vision and mantra.

There is no one "right" meeting cadence. The cadence depends on your culture. Be prepared to learn and improve. If your team is living the mantra and your business is achieving its goals, moving toward your vision, communication is most probably on track.

Besides communication cadence, another consideration is your method of communication. Are you going to use texting or a messaging app? Are you going to email? Are you going to communicate via remote meetings? Will you share video recordings? When will in-person meetings be critical? Keep these conversations happening with the team.

As an executive, if you are leading strategic planning, ensuring project management, and overseeing communication cadences, you can move mountains.

SYSTEMIZATION AND THE SUCCESS CYCLE

So far, I've been giving you a high-level view of your life at the top of your organization. But you've got to grow into it. Systemization is how you start. Systemization is just a way of looking at your business as a working system and then figuring out what that system needs to flourish. This is the tactical side of being and becoming a top-level executive, which I often refer to as the "Success Cycle."

1. **Define and document your vision.** Where do you want to be in the next year, five years, and ten years? What is your vision for the future of your business? Whatever it is, now is the time to get it down on paper. Moving things from your mind to written form is the first step toward transitioning from business owner to executive.

2. **Define what a successful result looks like.** Be specific. Revenue is an obvious example. Let's say you want to increase your revenue by x dollars. What will you do to make this happen?

3. **Determine what the drivers of that result are.** Revenue doesn't just magically happen in a dental practice. You have to have two things: (1) patients (read: patient flow—you have to have patients coming in the door) and (2) care—you're going to have to have clinicians who can provide appropriate care or treatments for those patients. These are the drivers of the revenue result.

4. **Determine the metric to measure the drivers.** How many patients came in? That's a metric. How much care was provided to them? That's another metric, which is measured in dollars.

5. **Determine how often to look at metrics.** How often should they be measured? Hourly? Daily? Weekly? Monthly? Measure your most important metrics daily, then determine which can be measured weekly or monthly.

6. **Determine how to automate the creation of the metrics.** Dashboards and other technology solutions are critical to enabling the team to clearly understand what their goals are.

7. **Decide how your team should respond to the various metrics.** What are the actions the team can take to influence the driver and make it better?

8. **Build the documents that train your team to understand the metrics.** The training needs to explain the whys of what they see, the drivers of the results, and the results themselves. It should also include actions to take based on those results.

9. **Put all the training together.** Roll it out to your team.

There you have it: the Success Cycle!

Despite how specific these steps are and the detail that goes into creating them, it's important to remember that you are growing into a generalist instead of remaining a specialist, by virtue of being a clinician and entrepreneur. You are becoming a top-level executive, a transformational leader who influences and impacts the lives of others on a grander scale. This readies you for your next step: building a great DSO. We'll embark on DSOs in the next chapter.

SOME GOOD READING

Remember that passion for learning you developed to become a top-level business owner? Well, it doesn't go away. As you enter this next stage, there are five books I recommend.

Extreme Ownership: How US Navy SEALS Lead and Win by Jocko Willink and Leif Babin. In Extreme Ownership, the authors reinforce what it means to be an executive and have the right kind of mindset to reach the next level. I have all my executives read this and the other books to gain the insights they need in order to know how to lead at the highest level. There's a mindset this book lays out that is hard to find in other books. No excuses.

The Dichotomy of Leadership: Balancing the Challenges of Extreme Ownership to Lead and Win also by Jocko Willink and Leif Babin. In this book, the authors address all the dichotomies you're dealing with constantly. These might include asking yourself, Do I help them? Do I not help them? What's the best course of action here? When do I step up to set the vision? When do they set the vision? Your whole leadership life seems like the choice between two great or two bad options. Jocko and Leif do a good job of breaking down the dichotomies.

The Goal: A Process of Ongoing Improvement, thirtieth anniversary edition, by Eliyahu M. Goldratt and Jeff Cox, is a book about identifying your key constraints and then prioritizing what to work on next. This book has given me an edge that many executives and entrepreneurs lack. Most leaders can see the vision but can't see the prerequisites that need to be accomplished first or the constraints that must be overcome before getting to that vision. This book will help tremendously.

Crucial Conversations: Tools for Talking When Stakes Are High, second edition, by Kerry Patterson, Joseph Grenny, Ron McMillan, and Al Switzler, explains how crucial conversations feel from a physiological perspective and how to ensure you are prepared for them. To have a productive conversation, even when it's difficult, you must bring your best self to it and see the opportunity. Leadership is all about our ability to communicate. Communication is our only real tool as our business scales. This book gives you the power to be a little better at it.

Finally, *Radical Candor: Be a Kick-Ass Boss without Losing Your Humanity* by Kim Scott. Having worked at Google and Apple, Kim has a great perspective on building amazing executive leadership. She breaks leaders into four quadrants. I was humbled after reading this book, and it gave me a path for improvement I am still working on. This book, like the others, has been life-changing for me.

CHAPTER 6

Don't Build
an Evil DSO

It's Pretty Easy Not To

I've always loved the branding name Dental Support Organization. It seems to lay out exactly what the industry needs—dentists as the first priority, with a supporting organization behind them. The best DSOs support all the business functions of running a practice, thus ensuring the dentist maintains the highest level of autonomy to focus on the clinical needs of patients.

Yet there tends to be two types of dental entrepreneurs: those who are willing to trust a DSO and those who aren't. The latter are wary of DSOs because they've heard stories that have convinced them that DSOs are controlling and "evil." That's not how I think of them. I call these organizations DCOs—Dental Control Organizations. Don't be a DCO.

These worries of controlling and evil DCOs have scared many a dentist-entrepreneur. I think this fear is unwarranted. Dentists are the customer. If DSOs are to succeed, it will be by creating value for their customer. All DSOs that start to exhibit DCO qualities are quickly called out by their dentists, and soon they must either switch back to a DSO value-creation model or see their team's turnover skyrocket until they are economically destroyed.

DSOs are servant-leaders. They follow the vision of the chief dental officer (CDO) or chief clinician of the board.

Great DSOs start with correct values. Great DSOs don't control; they support their most important customer, and the customers of a DSO are its clinicians. The support of clinicians must drive the strategic planning, focus, and priorities of a DSO. In this way, a great DSO—a great Dental Support Organization—earns its name.

WHAT IS A DSO EXACTLY?

From a legal perspective, a DSO forms when stakeholders set up an LLC or some other entity that sits next to a PLLC and provides management services to those entities. DSOs are reimbursed for their services, thereby also acting as a vehicle to move the economics of the practice up to the LLC. This allows nonclinicians to have ownership in the economic success of supporting the practice.

This is a mutually beneficial arrangement. A clinician who wants to scale or to gain the full value of their hard work and effort eventually has a financial need that can be best solved through banks and investors. Investors can support the expansion of healthcare and dentistry by participating in economic outcomes through their investment. And this investment enables a very necessary executive team to oversee business functions that must be brought in to transform a dental practice into a larger-scale entity. This increases the impact a dental practice can have in expanding patient care. The bottom line for the dentist is that a DSO structure means serving more patients while creating a growing financial enterprise.

ALIGNING WITH THE CLINICAL VISION

One of the biggest mistakes I've seen clinicians make as they transition to DSO leadership is not understanding their various hats. Some of the worst DSOs have been led by dentists who have a high desire to care for the patient but don't appreciate the importance of caring for their new customer: the associate. They still see themselves as a practice owner who can "boss around" the dentists, or they take an apathetic approach and let the dentists do whatever they want. Neither of these approaches would be called "leading with vision."

One of the most critical items any DSO executive can do is get clear on the clinical vision of the chief dental officer and clinical leadership. If the clinical leadership does not have a clear vision of who they want to serve, start by helping them develop a clinical vision document. This will be the North Star for leading and developing your DSO team.

Remember that the patient is now the customer of your customer. The customers of a DSO are the clinicians. Their vision of patient access, patient care, and patient engagement will drive the entire success of the organization. Help them develop and scale their ACE vision.

CLINICIAN SUPPORT IN STEPS

Three steps let CEOs support clinicians:

1. Help the chief dental officer or chief medical officer create a vision for patient access, care, and engagement. The more this can be documented and defined, the greater the alignment and support the DSO can bring.

2. Gather the right data. Often clinical leadership doesn't lead well because it doesn't have the right data to have the right conversations. Talking clinically is like talking about politics or religion. Data can be a great harmonizer. Bring data into every conversation and ask questions.

3. Communicate humbly. With a clear vision and clear data, you are all set to listen. Yes, this is the time to ask questions. Questions around the vision and where you are and are not aligned as an organization and how to get there. Questions around the data and why certain clinicians are below average and why some are above. (Pro insight: per the definition of averages, 50 percent of people will always be below average.) The goal is to constantly be looking for the next way to support, not criticize, to push out more resources, not blame.

Step 1: Align the CEO and CDO

When the CEO and CDO get together to align, they'll need to decide matters such as the following:

- What do we want our clinicians to achieve, and what support do they need in order to get there?

- Culturally, what behaviors are most important to them?

- Who is the patient we are most interested in serving?

- What capabilities do our doctors need in order to serve those patients?

- What investments are we going to make this year to help support our clinicians and their teams?

These questions can lead to an overall clinical strategic mission and DSO alignment. For example, when hiring doctors or having a doctor meeting, the CDO might say, "Our aim is to serve this patient type, and these capabilities are critical to have in order to serve this patient type." Then the CEO, in their meeting, may say, "Our mission as a DSO is to support our clinicians in serving these patient types and ensuring they have the resources they need to develop and be supported in these clinical capabilities."

The CEO also defines core foundations, such as the following, that make for a more successful enterprise:

- A documented clinical vision in coordination with the chief dental officer

- A clear strategic vision for the DSO to support the clinicians

- The culture the DSO must develop to support a larger team

- The systems and technology needed to increase patient experience and improve doctor support

Once these have been established and defined, it's time to layer in data and metrics, remembering that the DSO CEO doesn't operate from a strictly financial perspective but now has context in supporting the clinical vision and the CDO in their leadership.

Step 2: Gather the Right Data

As a team, you must start by defining which clinical metrics are important for your clinical and operations team to be successful. For example, you might use the American Dental Association (ADA), the American Association of Orthodontics (AAO), the American Academy of Pediatric Dentistry (AAPD), or other professional clinical associations' recommended ratios for a baseline to help you determine ratios for clinical leadership.

In gathering data, you might ask these questions:

- What is our patient flow by hygiene, treatment, and specialty? Is this sufficient patient flow for the doctors, or do we need to do more in marketing?

- Which treatment plans are completed the same day? Which treatment plans are completed within thirty days?

- How well are we collecting by insurance type? What is the timing of our accounts receivable collections?

- What amount of care are doctors doing at each visit? If we analyze this by age, insurance type, or appointment type, does it tell us how to better support our doctors and where potential bottlenecks are?

By using data and knowing the numbers, we can have a more educated conversation around the care needed and the care being delivered. The clinician might offer feedback about things to consider or inspect when looking at the data. You can then gather those data points and determine if they indicate best practices or if there are other improvements that need to be made.

Remember, we're ultimately dealing with humans, so there's more to think about than just numbers—but the numbers can direct us in how best to support our humans.

Step 3: Communicate Humbly with Support as the Goal

We learned how important communication is to the clinician in Chapter 1. It's important for those on the operational side of things too. The CEO of the DSO must make sure clinicians feel that the business side is helping them to reach goals and treat more patients more effectively. Clinicians enter the industry to take care of patients, so CEOs must communicate that this priority is also the priority of the DSO. Since the DSO is centered on supporting the clinician's goals, listening and learning are important leadership skills that go a long way toward creating alignment.

SUPPORT SYSTEMS

Some people interpret supporting clinicians as giving the clinicians full autonomy and not really mentoring or supporting them. Others believe support equals telling clinicians what to do. This points to a CEO who ignores the uniqueness of the dental industry.

I define supporting clinicians as giving them complete support to reach their goals and the goals of the clinical vision established by the Chief Dental Officer.

You have to find that balance between clinician autonomy and consistent, meaningful mentorship. There's always a conversation to be had around standard of care in dentistry: if dentistry is a science, we should all be able to agree on how to calculate that standard of care and how to create a model with predictability and therefore scalability.

This is truly a partnership between the chief clinician and the business professional CEO. If they are one in the same, make sure you are doing both well. Establish a vision for each to follow.

A WORD OF WARNING FOR CLINICIANS AND BUSINESS PROFESSIONALS ENTERING A DSO PARTNERSHIP

For clinicians: It is human nature to resist feedback. It's human nature to sometimes not be self-aware. It's human nature to put defenses up. Throwing up defenses is almost always a sign there are things we need to analyze. When you want to snap, "You're not a clinician. You don't understand," it's time to step back.

If someone is telling you how to treat your patients and what kind of procedure you should provide to each patient, then there is a case for using your defense shield of your specialized education. But if someone is advising you to help you improve your skills for stronger leadership or is sharing data to help you advance your clinical capability for better patient care overall, then take it as a blessing of continuing education.

For business professionals: Clinicians throughout the enterprise are much more than employees. They work on the health of human beings with hard-won professional expertise. Meanwhile, they deal with the complexities of human nature on a day-to-day basis. Though clinicians may try to explain to business professionals the reality and nuances of what they face and need, the business professionals—having not been through dental school—may find it hard to understand.

But they need to. How else can they provide appropriate support? So they need to listen as clinicians give them feedback. They need to reassess their data points on those variables that could be affecting their analysis. And, in general, they must remember the concept of servant leadership.

If everyone checks their ego at the door, the opportunities for growth and quality patient care are tremendous.

Now, armed with the clarity of your why, the power of the ACE, entrepreneur and executive leadership skills, knowing the dangers of the Dark Tunnel, and knowing what it truly means to support clinicians, you are ready to build your DSO.

And now that we know that a successful DSO remembers that the clinician is the customer and its function is support, you may be wondering if it's time for you to move into a DSO. If you come to the answer of yes, I have provided the rest of the book to give you the nuts and bolts of building a DSO. Feel free to read these chapters in the order that you need. And good luck on your journey of personal development.

Additional resources found here:

IT'S TIME FOR THE NUTS AND BOLTS

After holding master classes on Facebook Live for people dreaming of or worried about starting a DSO, we've found that the same questions come up repeatedly. Consistent, smart questions that dentist-entrepreneurs ask most often include discussions on financing, accounting processes, hiring systems, and how to create a great customer experience. Given how important these questions are, I'm dedicating the next chapters to these nuts and bolts.

Again, I can't cover in one book every circumstance you, in particular, will face. As I said early on, this book is meant to give you only an overview, a basic "here's the lay of the land you'll see along your entrepreneurial journey." I know that will leave you with a lot of unanswered questions, especially as you experience the stages of your own journey. That's why we created the DSO Facebook group and the podcast, and joined on with the Dentist Entrepreneur Organization: to give dentist-entrepreneurs a chance to connect with peers and executives and

more deeply investigate the burning questions dentist-entrepreneurs always have. And of course you can talk to trusted
mentors in your own life.

But I can start answering some of your nuts-and-bolts questions right here. In the next chapter, we're going to cover a
crucial question dentists should ask first in the DSO phase:
how can we provide an amazing customer experience?

CHAPTER 7

Creating an Amazing Customer Experience

Well, in the first place, you've got to understand who your customer is. Seems obvious, right? But in dentistry, and healthcare generally, it can get complicated quickly.

If you have been to any of my presentations, you know that I am passionate about understanding the customer and have a little fire in my belly when a dentist answers the question "Who is your customer?" with "I just do bread-and-butter dentistry." That is not a customer!

Many dentists and groups are getting better at this. Some dentists now at least say things like, "My customers are geriatric patients in South Florida who need implants quickly." Okay, that's better. Some identify children as their primary focus.

Other dentists claim the customers "who are too terrified to get work done without specific accommodations" as their patients. These are all headed in the right direction.

If you've identified your main patient avatar (*avatar* means a representation of your ideal customer) and have improved your business to serve their unique needs, I tip my hat to you. It means that there's a good chance your marketing is successfully reaching them and that your clinicians know how to treat your patients once they come in.

But none of the people coming through your doors are now your direct customers. Not when you are wearing your new DSO hat.

Your customers are now your clinicians. You are there to *support them*, and not just passively, but actively.

The patients? They are now the customers of your customers. When you support clinicians in every way you can to make their job easier, freeing them to provide *their* customers amazing experiences, then you will have succeeded.

THE DSO MINDSET: SUPPORT

In a real sense, you've been a Dental Support Organization since you hired your first associate. That associate came to work with you because they expected that doing so would mean that you would handle the marketing strategy, HR support, IT needs, compliance education, and everything else that goes into running the business of the practice. They also expected that you would provide them some level of mentoring and guidance to grow as a clinician. These are all the support elements of a great DSO.

Unfortunately, for many dentist-entrepreneurs, hiring the associate to function within their practices is the end of the support. That's because, instead of extending support to their associates, dentists often hire other associates with the mindset that the associates will support them.

Dentists commonly make this mistake since they are overwhelmed entrepreneurs trying to grow a business. They want and hire help because they feel justifiably swamped, confused, and worried. They're at the center of their hub-and-spoke enterprise, everything depending on them. It's easy to stay stuck in that pressurized, overworked mindset when it's time to start making the mindset shift toward supporting.

I once heard the story of a practice owner who brought his associate to the top of a beautiful hill overlooking a beautiful piece of land. There was a large, expensive house, nice vehicles in the driveway, and horses running in the pasture. The practice owner turned to the associate and said, "If you work really hard, I mean really increase your capability, put in the long hours, and sacrifice often for the good of the practice, someday all of this could be mine." This is not the right mindset.

Moving into a new supportive mindset means embracing servant leadership. It means changing the mindset such that you see the practice team and associates as your primary customers. It means acknowledging that some people in your practice should be trained up to take on leadership roles and that your role is to facilitate and support. It means moving from being a day-to-day workhorse to being a leader. It means lowering the anxiety and increasing the confidence.

In this new way of functioning, you'll be tasked to start thinking of such things as the following:

- Do my clinicians have what they need to do their best today, this week, this month, this quarter, and this year? *not* They better be good because I pay them a lot of money.

- What projects are we working toward that will provide our associates additional support? *not* I don't have time to support them; I'm too busy taking care of my own patients.

- How can I create, shape, and communicate my vision to each associate to expand our reach of patient care? *not* If they want to talk to me or need help, then they can book a meeting with me.

- And, most importantly, Why should a doctor come work with us instead of somewhere else or on their own?

not If a doctor isn't smart enough to know a good thing when they see it, then I don't want them here.

As you look over this list, you may want to choose one area that could use a little more attention from you today.

YOUR VALUE OFFERING FOR ASSOCIATES

Whether or not your associates are going to be heroes for their customers is mostly on you—on how well you serve *your* customer, the associate. A critical part of making sure your associate is an ACE clinician is aligning your associate to the customers of your practice. Then you must start asking (and never stop asking), "How do I support you, my associate, in creating a great positive impact on your patients?"

Your associates want that support. That's why they're coming to work with you. They expect that you know how to do the billing, that you're compliant, that your finances are in order, that you have a good marketing strategy, and so on. They dream you're going to walk them into their future by modeling how a successful practice runs. They would ultimately love to partner with you and build their own passive income stream.

Don't let their expectations and yours drift far apart. Dentist-entrepreneurs may think, *I'm finally hiring an employee! I'm paying their salary so they'll do what I say and relieve some of my pressure.* The associate, meanwhile, expects that their position means no pressure; they're just coming in to practice what they learned in dental school or to "finally only have to do dentistry." From an associate's perspective, they're doing all this production but only getting a percentage. The rest of the percentage is "paid" to you because they see you as providing goods and services. Associates do expect a return, whether they've clearly articulated it or not. Figuring out how to provide that return so that associates feel supported and at their best is your first priority.

To do that, you must think a lot about what value you offer. Take the time to sit down and ask yourself some questions around your value offering:

- Why would a clinician come work with our team?

- What do we provide to them?

- Is the location of my practice in a place where associates want to live and work?

- Is there something about my culture, the compensation, the level of support, the patient type, the procedures, or clinical capability that associates will desire?

- Does my combination of offerings set me apart from other places they could work?

- Am I giving them what they need and want to do their best?

- Am I giving them enough value and support that they don't benefit from going elsewhere to work?

Just like any other customers, your associates will be constantly weighing the benefits of what you offer against the marketplace in general. (As an aside, this is why I believe DSOs will greatly benefit clinicians. The market will continue to compete, bringing more and more value to them!)

It's not that you have to be a ten out of ten on all of those questions, but you must understand the facts of your value offering. If you're a five out of ten on one question, you're going to need to be better on others. For instance, we support some practices in rural towns, but many people want to live in or near large metropolitan areas. If you're like us, then you're going to have to bring massive value with your culture, compensation, and mentoring.

RECRUITING ASSOCIATES

Sometimes we use the term *recruiting* as if it's a unique, separate department. But the reality is that *recruiting* is just a fancy word for "marketing and sales" from the HR department.

As practice owners, we put a lot of time and energy into finding marketing teams to help us with patient acquisition. To recruit associates, you just put the exact same focus, energy, and methods into doctor acquisition. Have you done this?

- Are you focusing the same attention on social media for doctor recruiting as you are for patient recruiting?

- Does your website speak to associates and their needs as a customer?

- Do you have brochures for your practices that show the benefits of each practice and why someone would want to work there?

If you feel that marketing is outside your capability, let me give you a simple place to start: decide what the key pain points of your customers are. What things in the marketplace that associates need or want are they not getting? For instance, if dentists are worried about student loan repayments, is there something you can do there? If they're worried about having support in their clinical capability, is there something you can do for them there? If they aspire to leadership positions, can you provide a path for that? If there's a certain amount of leadership they *don't* want to have to do, can you support them there? By thinking in terms of marketing to your future associates as customers, your sophistication improves.

Of course, you're not trying to get every dentist. You want the right people for your practices. You need to define your customer avatar (ideal customer attributes). For simplicity, I'll divide dentists into two categories of avatar. One type is the entrepreneurial dentist who is looking to aggressively grow their capability. They want to work long hours, and they want to eventually be owners. Will you be able to satisfy those ambitions? Will you be able to give them complex cases and support them in learning new capabilities? Will you be able to give them a partnership program at some point?

Then there's the associate looking for stability. They might not be as aggressive about clinical capability, but they're extremely loyal. They want consistency and simplicity. They want a talented and stable team. They want compensation that does not vary much. Will you provide that?

Of course, like any customer, associates may want everything under the sun, but how are they prioritizing their wants? You should know and document your value offering to associates.

Are you going for "shooting stars"—the highly ambitious, never satisfied clinician—or are you looking for "rock stars"—the highly stable, less-open-to-change clinician?

Another growing group of dentists wants to work part-time or shifts. Fifty-one percent of some dental school graduating classes are female, a huge shift in the industry from thirty years ago. Generally speaking, the data shows that the number of hours women want to work is about 80 percent of what their male counterparts want to work. Can you offer shifts within your practice to support these doctors?

After you figure out who you're looking for and what you can offer them, you'll need to create traditional marketing material. You'll need a dedicated website that tells how you're going to help this customer—this dentist. You might use landing pages and social media teams; all the things you think about when it comes to patient acquisition, you need to think about for doctor acquisition.

And, of course, once you successfully recruit them, you must work to retain them through your support. Give them an amazing customer experience.

Supporting your clinician customers so that they can give their own customers amazing experiences should give you the confidence to become a top-level DSO.

Which brings you to the next common question: should I build a DSO from scratch (de novo) or acquire existing practices? We'll cover that in the next chapter.

CHAPTER 8

Business Development

Build New or Acquire?

Should you build your DSO from the ground up? Or should you acquire an existing practice or practices?

It's a big decision, this acquisition versus de novo (Latin meaning "from the new"). With the acquisition model, you inherit existing patient rosters, employees, and an established entity. You have cash flow and consistency on day one. It also means, of course, that you must navigate and integrate into an existing culture, procedures, technology, and so on.

You'll also need to decide whether all your facilities are going to be standardized. Transitioning an acquired practice into yours or vice versa creates noise and turbulence, at least temporarily. And here's where your experience with creating an amazing experience for your customer—that is, your clinicians—positions you to make informed decisions. For one thing, how can you uphold your record of great customer experiences in the face of a transition for them? How can you provide the people you bring on board a consistently great experience? You can't just assume people will adjust. This support role is your job and the job of those you have hired or will hire. How will you support them to have the best experience so that they, in turn, will provide the best experience to their customers? Blending ingredients, of course, doesn't always result in winning combinations. In fact, blending some materials makes explosives. Best to avoid that.

With de novo, you don't have to worry about many of the above. You get to design your own facility, choose your equipment, hire your own people, and see your vision come to life. As great as that may sound, you won't have any patients when you open. And you will have incredible financing challenges. It's much easier to get financing for a new acquisition than for something to be built from the ground up.

So which is best? There is no "right" answer. Ultimately, the decision comes down to what your vision is for your DSO and what inherent challenges you're willing to create solutions for. This is definitely an opportunity to choose your own entrepreneurial adventure based on your and your team's strengths and weaknesses, resources and deficits.

ACQUIRING: PROS AND CONS

Remember that we are in an evolving industry that is still consolidating. Right now, the majority of dentists seeking to expand or build a Dental Support Organization are focused on acquisition opportunities. Those going this route know that dentists preparing to retire may be looking for someone to take over the day-to-day operations while the retiring dentists begin to step back. They know that many dentists are looking for additional support and want to maximize the equity of their practice. In these situations, both parties win in an acquisition strategy. A DSO can ease the transition, while the acquiring dentist gets a built-in patient flow in an established location.

And these practices are proven models. They are producing revenue and have a certain customer base used to receiving a certain standard of care. They have staff and historical budget data. Because they are going concerns (accounting talk for businesses that are profitable), obtaining financing is much easier.

Of course—and here come the cons—the profitable nature of a well-run potential acquisition means it can command a premium. The cost might mean you can't get financing for the whole deal. Earn-outs and other sophisticated financing solutions may be necessary to make the deal happen. Your legal and financial support will need to be talented to complete some of these deals.

Dentists who don't have the capital may instead buy poorly performing practices. In fact, they may buy several to expand quickly. There are a few cons here. Getting ten or so locations is great for the sense of forward momentum and even ego. But it's another matter to transform these acquisitions into well-run and profitable practices. Typically, a handful at most begin to perform well. The rest don't unless turning around struggling practices is a specific skill you've developed within your team.

Remember that you're not just buying some building with an immediate stream of income thanks to patient flow. Humans come along with this practice, which means you inherit an existing practice's strengths, weaknesses, and cultural dysfunctions. You inherit the practice's facility design, equipment, compliance processes, and software solutions. What you do with all this can make or break your own business. A poorly performing or even great practice needs its weaknesses shored up and eliminated, from people to processes. Are you up for that?

In the world of finance, there's a concept called a J-curve. It indicates that after you buy something and then implement your culture and systems, its revenue and profitability drop a bit before they can go up. This needs to be something you have financially prepared for. In a worst-case scenario, revenue and profitability can go down and never come back up again.

Let me give one specific scenario to watch for. I've seen and experienced acquisitions where the culture was poor and the sellers were not completely honest with their teams. They weren't even compliant. And yet they were profitable.

Okay, I thought, *I'll come in with our systems, our amazing culture, and our robust compliance program. We'll get this practice in tip-top shape in no time.* My confidence grew as I imagined they'd shout our praises once they could see the error of their previous owners' ways and become the well-run team they had dreamed of becoming. But soon I hit a wall and learned a hard lesson: dysfunction breeds dysfunction.

It hadn't occurred to me to ask why the doctors and staff had stayed on despite their less-than-ideal working conditions. As we brought in what we considered a more functional, healthier environment, people started opting out. Long-term, that wasn't bad at all, but in the short term, when we were trying to switch things over, having people opting out and replacing them caused turbulence. It then took even longer to get our own systems and people in place. Profitability dropped quickly. A situation like this can create longer than expected J-curves.

We did absorb the drop and rebound in profitability. Change did happen eventually. I'm proud that we were able to take a practice that wasn't operating as ethically or as compliantly as we'd like and turn it around. Now it's a high-performing practice. But it's not for the faint of heart.

DE NOVO: PROS AND CONS

If you're not sure you want to inherit the good with the bad through acquiring a practice, a de novo practice might be looking pretty good. You're not going to walk in and find something built in 1980 with staff still using paper charts and a facility falling apart.

Instead, you start with a blank slate, your vision built into everything. You choose the real estate and the facility design, hire people on day one, and have them all trained on the system and processes you have decided to put in place. Going the de novo route puts you in control every step of the way.

I think those going de novo tend to have some of the best business models out there. Instead of buying somebody else's success, they think deeply in advance about the needs of the customer and the practice as dictated by their vision. They recruit the doctors and staff they need, get the right equipment for their niche, and know where to put their practice to ensure nearly immediate patient flow. They can go where their customers are and design every aspect of their model to take care of their customers.

Of course, going de novo takes more marketing prowess and patient-customer clarity than acquiring does, a possible downside for some. The core question for most de novo wannabes is "How will I ramp up patient flow?"

GROWING A DE NOVO PATIENT FLOW

If you are going the de novo route, it's because you feel you have something special. You have data from a best practice that you want to duplicate. You may have built the first locations largely from intuition, but now you need to formalize and systemize the process.

From a patient's first visit, begin tracking how often they return and which types of patients are most likely to return for which procedure needs. You want to know which patients will be most attracted to your product and keep track of them. This is a two-step process. You've got to get them in the door, and then you've got to ensure they keep coming back. The data is in your practice management software; you'll need to analyze it. This software has incredible sets of information on who is coming in and how often, and which patient types are most attracted to your brand and clinical service.

Now that you know your ideal patient, you can use psychographic software and tools to identify where they are in the cities and towns where you want to build. You can find the locations within those towns where they are most likely to be, and then do your best to build close to those pathways of travel.

You will also want to build a pro forma financial statement—a financial projection of how the practice is doing. The more often you do this, the better you'll get at it. Two big things could change your projections:

- **The patient flow component/quotient:** Do you put more money into marketing and hope things will ramp up more quickly or do you manage costs tightly and wait long enough to gain a profit? And in either case, where does that money come from?

- **Associates falling short of projections:** Your new associates may or may not perform treatments equal to what you put on the pro forma. Maybe patients have needs that your associates aren't comfortable doing or the associates aren't comfortable with a particular age group or demographic. You'll need to be prepared to support your associates in this growth.

If you're in a new location trying to ramp up patient flow with a clinician who doesn't have confidence, where do you get the money to provide training and mentoring? Doing projections lets you find discrepancies between expectation and reality and move to solve problems while they're virtual and small.

A big challenge of going de novo is clearly the financing. It's hard to convince a bank that their money is safe when you're starting from scratch. New builds can be unpredictable if you're the new guy in town. Without enough historical data and size, you won't be able to give them the confidence they need to provide you the capital. Because traditional banks don't like to work with entrepreneurial startups, if you choose to do a new-build model, you might want to find a nonbank lender. You may even need something like a mezzanine loan. Though it comes with a much higher interest rate, it may be your only path to scale your vision.

Or you might look into an equity partner—a private equity or venture capital firm that believes in your ability to succeed. And, of course, you can beg, borrow, and steal (don't steal!) from family, friends, and other dentists to get yourself up and running to show that the model you have really works. Personally, I did all of the above when we were starting out. Once you prove yourself, purse strings will loosen a little and more people will be willing to give you money. But this won't happen overnight. It's a slow process, but worth it for those who have a specific vision they want to bring to the market-place.

OTHER INFLUENTIAL FACTORS

Knowing about the pros and cons of acquiring versus de novo business development is about matching the best and worst to your own skillset.

Are these your strengths? You want to go the acquisition route. You or someone on your executive team has the ability to lead an existing practice through integration and onboarding into your organization. You love assessing new teams and inte-grating various cultures. You can get different personalities aligned and create a cohesive vision. You love the complexity of various service offerings and can see the important thread connecting them all.

Or are these your strengths? You want to start something from scratch. You know the customer type you want to serve and a specific way you want to serve them. You know customers will love having something different in the marketplace. You love assessing locations that will serve the customer type you want. You are amazing at marketing strategy. You have lots of access to capital or don't mind hunting it down. This is something you can see yourself and your team doing well.

Your skills and those of your team must suit your choice of acquisition or de novo.

Besides your available skillset, other factors are in play. Timing, logistics, circumstances in your personal life, market constraints—such considerations are the context for your decision. You've got to consider the realities around you to give yourself the best chance of making a good decision, one that will create more success on your own terms. For instance, if you're playing a longer game, there's no need to build out quickly. You may opt to build quality locations under a single brand in order to do things the way you've developed for your existing locations. You've created a proven model that works, and if it takes longer to do because this way is slower to finance, so be it. Or, if you're wanting to move faster and have a platform that can service many different practice types, you may want to acquire.

The point is that to make the right decision, your circumstances and available skillsets must be added to the scales as you weigh the pros and cons of de novo or acquiring. Inventory your skills and resources. Consider your challenges, gaps, and business vulnerabilities. Consider the timing and strength you will personally need to bring to bear. The decision can't merely be reduced to numbers, like which choice nets the most equity. The right decision comes down to you. This is a "choose your own adventure" experience.

In the next chapter, we're going to discuss some of the questions that come up on different financing options and learn some new jargon.

CHAPTER 9

Financing Your Dreams into Reality

Debt and Investment

As members of the transforming, consolidating dental industry, our business journey can have some surprising twists and turns, especially when it comes to financing. Imagine this scenario:

A dentist walks into a bank and says, "Listen, I just got out of school. I'm drowning in debt and my personal balance sheet doesn't look like I'm worth lending to, but I want to buy a practice. The practice is $400,000."

You have no experience in business, but the dental industry has a very low default rate. The default rate is something like 0.5 percent.

The banker says, "No problem. Sign here!" In some cases, you could have a loan in as little as three days.

Congratulations! You bought your first practice. Now what?

You want to do a good job with it, which means profits. But do you know how to run a practice? Do you know how to work with a practice manager? Do you know how to manage an X-ray tech?

No.

You're going to have tons of stress in your life. Your income is going to be low, and you'll have to take from your personal income to pay down that $400,000 debt. The banker knows this and has figured out that, over time, you can make sure the bank gets paid just using your hands.

You work hard and you get really good. In fact, you've become somewhat of an expert on your business. It came more naturally than you thought it would, and you grew your practice within six months. The practice you bought for $400,000 is worth $2 million. Brilliant! You're on a roll! You figure with such a return, you should be golden at the bank. And you're ready to add a new practice.

You go back to the bank and say, "Listen, I want to do this again! Look at what I've been able to do with the first loan. I understand a lot more now. I've figured out how to run a practice and work with a practice manager. I know how to bring patients in. I can run the staff and negotiate with vendors. Oh, and the numbers—I've got my accounting up to snuff. Each line item is accounted for...so, can I borrow more money?"

The banker narrows their eyes, studying you. "Um, let's wait a little bit and see what happens. Come back in a couple years, once this loan is paid down more." Or, if you're lucky, you might hear, "Absolutely! Go ahead. You can do one more."

This is what you wanted to hear. You can move forward on your second practice. Six months later, your second practice is also doing $2 million, so you think to yourself, *Wow, I'm really on a roll. I'm ready and able to add another practice.*

You go to the bank and say, "I've done it again! I've got this great new opportunity for a third practice location. Can I borrow again?"

The bank says, "No. No more."

You're stunned. *What? Why won't they give me a third loan?* you wonder. *They gave one to me when I started out, drowning in student debt and fresh out of school. What gives?*

Then your buddy, who has just graduated from dental school, goes to the bank for a loan. He gets the okay from the banker. What's going on here?

TRANSITIONING INDUSTRY
AND TRADITIONAL BANKING

The banking industry is traditional. Our industry isn't. It has moved away from individual mom-and-pop cottage-industry dental practices. No one thought about dentists having more than one location and certainly not enterprise-level numbers of up to thirty locations! Including bankers. Their banking system and process is not made for the DSO world.

If you have one or two locations, you're still considered a mom-and-pop shop. What the banks figured out long ago is that you, as a dentist, have the means and the skills to work your way out of any loan, so with little to no experience, you can get a loan and start buying or building a practice.

By practice three or sometimes a few more, you're no longer the owner of an individual practice but a business owner. You need management skills for your multilocation practices, and the money you need is probably a couple million instead of just the half million you needed when you didn't have to budget in such things as IT systems, sophisticated marketing, and HR departments. The investment and risk, in a banker's mind, are higher.

The checklist the traditional bankers have established for your type of business doesn't fit our transitioning industry anymore. They have boxes to tick and federal guidelines to follow. They have a maximum range they're comfortable loaning to an individual dentist with the full knowledge that it's a personally guaranteed loan. If your practice falls apart, then the bank knows you can just go work for someone else and pay back your debt. What a bank is initially doing is underwriting your ability to make personal income and use that income to pay the debt.

But as you start to grow bigger, your ability to use your wages to pay back the loan dwindles. That's the heart of the problem. As you get more successful, banks are no longer looking at your clinical skills but instead scrutinizing your business skills. While the bank trusts that you can pay back a single loan or two with the skills you learned in dental school, scaling puts you in uncharted territory. This takes you from business owner banking to corporate finance.

SIDENOTE: FINANCIAL MISTAKES IN ACQUISITIONS

It's important to know how the banks determine their loans so you can avoid a mistake that most dentists—and even banks— make. Most banks make initial dental practice loans based on top-line revenue. Top-line revenue, or a percentage of it, is essentially where banks determine their own risk. Assuming your practice is doing $1 million and your loan is 80 percent, your practice loan would be $800,000.

Now let's look at your bottom line. We're still talking about a $1 million practice. But let's subtract an appropriate wage for an associate once you get that additional practice. And what wage would you or do you draw now as an associate clinician? After you pay yourself, what's left at the bottom?

Let's say $250,000 annually is paid to the associate and $100,000 will be left at the bottom to pay back the $800,000 loan. Using this math (and no interest rate, to keep it simple), and assuming all bottom-line income was used to pay down the loan, it would take you eight years to pay back the loan (800,000/100,000 = 8). What if the bottom line is $50,000? It will now take sixteen years to pay back the loan, or, more than likely, it will require you to eat into the associate's or owner's income to pay back the loan on time and not lose the practice.

The problem with stopping at top-line revenue when calculating practice value arises when you consider paying back an $800,000 loan. Early on, the banker does the math a little differently than you do. The banker thinks, *Oh, their wage is $250,000. I'm fine with that. It will only take this dentist four years to pay back the loan in the worst-case scenario.*

With a bottom line of $50,000 or $100,000, the ramifications are that fulfilling the bank's expectations means using your actual wages to pay the loan. That won't work if you actually want to eat, pay for your house, and travel. As a business owner, when considering financing a practice, start looking at your net income and ask yourself, *How long am I willing to spend paying back this loan that I want the bank to give me?* This will help you calculate a clearer value of the practice. Use this math when buying your second location and beyond. You won't have the luxury of taking the associate's wage to pay down the loan, so if there's no net income coming out of the practice, stay away from the purchase.

WHERE TO GET FINANCING

Given the chasm between the thinking of traditional bankers and that of the dentist member of a transitioning industry, you may be at a loss as to where to turn for financing when you're ready to scale.

One logical choice is to wait five to ten years until you pay down your existing loans. That means you can only open a practice once or twice a decade. Most people aren't satisfied with this pace, so I will provide a couple other creative options.

Buddy Up with a Dentist Looking to Open a Practice

When my business started in 2010, there were no real solutions when bankers refused to fund our successful de novos. We knew we wanted to retain our best doctors, and we knew they had an easier time getting loans than we did. So we decided to partner with the associates we trusted. That buddy fresh from dental school who doesn't have your years of hard-earned experience in practice can look great to a bank and Small Business

Administration lending. Here's how it can work: you partner with a dentist just beginning their practice, help them get the loan, figure out an equity split in a sub-DSO partnership, and provide them the resources as a DSO to increase their success. Now, understand that when you use this method to build out your dental empire, you'll end up with a lot of partners. You'll need a team that can bring real value and is great at communicating and training dentists on how to partner. It can be daunting, but it is a solution.

Turn to Your Assets and Network

Your friends and family might be willing to pitch in when you can't get financing. This can have relationship ramifications, so be cautious. Or sometimes a bank will lend you money as long as there's collateral. Again, be cautious. Your collateral can begin to feel like a hostage. That means a lot of stress as you work to pay off the loan. It can be equally stressful to rush to pay back friends and family who might also feel like the funds loaned to you are being held hostage. Early on, Dr. Chad Evans had family members putting up their family cabins as collateral in exchange for some equity in a sub-DSO entity. They put a lot on the line to ensure we were successful and could continue to grow. We had families with generational wealth that helped finance locations. This was stressful to manage but, in the end, allowed us to continue our growth until more sophisticated financing solutions were available.

Mezzanine Debt

When you've exhausted your options, there is one more kind of loan to consider: mezzanine debt. Mezzanine debt blurs the line between what debt is and what equity is. It's the highest-risk form of debt and offers some of the highest interest rates, but it can be worth considering.

Welcome to the world of investment banking. Remember that risk tolerance you said you had? Well, this is where the rubber meets the road, so to speak. Part of the reason you need strong nerves is that those involved in investment banking, and specifically mezzanine debt loans, aren't under traditional FDIC guidelines.

If you do get a mezzanine loan, be aware that your interest rate will be at least twice as much as—even three times more than—that of a traditional loan, putting you somewhere between 9 and 15 percent, and as high as 20 percent interest per year in some cases.

These rates allow investors and nontraditional lenders to be a bit more aggressive in what they lend, given that they are considered to be taking a greater risk on you. This can be a great solution because you can have a partner who wants to see you grow; it's a good return on investment for them to put more money in. But, as in any lending situation, it's important to use caution. Why? Because some of these lenders are unscrupulous and *want* you to not make your payments so they can then foreclose on your business and get it for a discount or even for free. Yikes.

Caution: Don't Break the Covenant

Covenants specify the ratios and factors you must meet in order for the bank to *not* foreclose on your business. Covenants are more than just "make your payments on time." In traditional small-business lending, covenants aren't always part of the agreement. But in larger-business banking they are, so I want to call them out here.

For example, if you buy a house and make your loan payments on time, that indicates you're doing well. In business, though, banks look at more indicators because business can get more complicated. Lenders want to get ahead of any issues you may create for yourself and may look at things like debt to EBITDA (pronounced "ee-bid-da") ratio. (We'll talk about EBITDA—earnings before interest, taxes, depreciation, and amortization—later.) Banks may look at the amount of debt you have versus the amount of EBITDA you have, and they'll have a limit on how much you can borrow based on how much EBITDA you have.

Here's an example of how EBITDA works:

Let's say you have $1 million of EBITDA. The bank says you can borrow up to $4 million, or four times your EBITDA number.

Great!

Except, here's the thing. When you borrowed your $4 million, you did it against your EBITDA of $1 million. But now you need to hire people to help you run your business. Once you subtract the costs of that plus insurance and FF&E (fixtures, furniture, and equipment), your EBITDA number has dropped to, say, $700,000.

Here's the dangerous part: if you were to go to the bank now, you'd actually only be able to borrow, say, $2.8 million. If you borrowed the $4 million, you're out of covenant. You've "broken" your agreement with the bank.

The bank can charge additional fees. They have the authority to send someone in to start taking over and running your business for you. They can even foreclose on you and sell all your assets to recoup their money. Banks will often try to work with you. Just be aware of what could happen. This scenario underlines why a strong CFO is so important. They can help you navigate the financing, especially if and when you find yourself getting into higher forms of investment such as senior lending, mezzanine lending, or equity.

USING EQUITY TO SCALE

Using equity to grow and scale your practice involves collaboration. Instead of taking loans from friends and family or mezzanine loans, you can partner with a private equity group (PE or PEG) so that they can "buy in" to your DSO structure and provide funds for scaling and growth.

If you want a PE partner, I'd suggest looking for private equity firms that have experience working with doctor-owned businesses. They should be familiar with your specific needs, especially your requirement to support clinicians to succeed. For instance, if they have invested in a healthcare technology company, that will have had an entirely different set of requirements than a customer-facing healthcare provider.

You'll also need to really assess their funding capacity. Can they grow with you, or will they run out of money? Equity firms have limits to how much they can put into each company. Once they hit the limit, their concentration risk is too high to continue funding your practice. This is an area where you want to be the small fish in a big pond. You want them to want to put more funds in as you need them, not be maxed out because you are the biggest investment in their portfolio.

THE CASE FOR A STRONG CFO

If you're ready to go down the financing path, I can't stress enough the importance of a strong CFO. For one thing, private equity, senior lending, and mezzanine debt lenders will want data and metrics. They will look through the keyhole of what the CFO provides them, not your whiteboard of vision and growth.

Additionally, you'll want the CFO's opinion of the best financing road to take. They'll be able to help you decide the best option for your business needs and be ready to manage the process.

Finally, your CFO can run point for you during board meetings. After all, mezzanine lenders or private equity partners often want to be on your board of directors. Depending on how much money they put into your business, they may even want control of the board. Ultimately, they will want to know how healthy your company is, how much money is coming in and going out, if you'll be able to pay back your loan, and more. They could have the right to fire you as CEO if they don't think you're running things correctly. This makes it imperative that you understand your investment relationship.

We'll talk more about your C-suite in the next two chapters, but it's worth calling out the CFO here. You need their help.

TAKING THE LEAP

People often ask me, "When is the best time to bring in a private equity firm or apply for a mezzanine debt loan?"

It's a judgment call you have to make. It has a lot to do with your personality and risk tolerance. While there's no magical formula, there are things you can look at to make the call. One of the biggest indicators is your growth strategy. Spend time with your CFO and map out various outcomes to determine if what you have in your head plays out on the spreadsheet. A CFO can help you measure some sensitivity analysis, such as "If this doesn't happen exactly as we plan, how bad does it get? What's the worst-case scenario? Would we break a covenant if we did this? Is what we are giving up in interest rate or equity going to be made up exponentially in our growth?"

Knowing more about your financing possibilities and their possible repercussions should make navigating this part of your business journey less daunting. Once you take this leap and begin to scale, you'll need to attend to your organizational chart. We'll cover that in the next chapter.

CHAPTER 10

Overview of an Organizational Chart

Hiring questions come up frequently when we give our master classes. Even though dentist-entrepreneurs already have experience with hiring, they have never built a team much beyond the dental practice. Early on, they may just need to get off the ground operationally. Are the candidates qualified? Yes? Great. Then the dentist-entrepreneurs plug them into roles and hope for the best.

But as they grow, so does their organizational chart, and they discover that writing out their chart and vision on a whiteboard is much more complex than before, and executing it is even harder. In a growing organization, issues such as alignment, teams, and capacity start mattering more and more.

So do mindset and personality. You need team members with new intense specialties and skillsets that still align with the company culture.

EXECUTIVES AND MIDDLE MANAGEMENT

Executives sit at the top of the organizational chart, providing strategic leadership and direction. I'll give a general perspective here and more detail in the next chapter.

DSOs generally have the same executives as other businesses. You've got your CEO, who runs the executive team and does a lot of work on the vision of the company. The CEO also searches out and interacts with investors. Your CFO will oversee finance, while the CMO works on marketing strategy. Remember that the *O* at the end of all these initialisms stands for *officer* and that the *C* always stands for *chief*: CTO, technology; CCO, compliance; COO, operations; and so on. All members of the C-suite deal with high-level matters such as outlining long-term strategies and putting them into practice through the managers answering to them. These leaders accomplish the longer-term goals through short-term goals and tactics implemented by those on the front lines of the business.

Depending on your needs and strategies, your DSO can create other C-suite executive positions. Maybe you need an executive to oversee HR in a high-level way because you believe that your future depends on hiring, firing, and developing a one-of-a-kind culture or because the DSO is entering a period of rapid scaling that calls for not only personnel but standardized training across many regions. Your C-suite executives are experts in their specialization. Their expertise means best practices become standard in your DSO.

The CDO—chief dental officer—will likely be you if you are a dentist reading this book. You learned how to think like an executive functioning as a CEO as you journeyed into this DSO phase. Since you (1) are a clinician by dental school training and have trained all the associates you hired, and (2) have also evolved into an executive with an understanding of the business side, it makes sense that you hold the CDO position. You have the key expertise and can talk the business side as well now, making you able to coordinate and communicate with the rest of the C-suite. Your vision will be critical for the DSO executives to know how best to support their doctor-customer.

You might, however, love the CEO position, executing visions and strategies at a high level. If so, you'll need a chief clinician to keep your business's clinical vision front and center. Every decision should be led by that mission. As mentioned earlier, we can take this on in more detail in the next chapter.

MIDDLE MANAGEMENT

DSOs tend to have two tiers of middle management. The first consists of practice managers who make sure that front-facing employees get what they need to do their job. You know these leaders well. They oversee day-to-day operations, dealing with not only the practice's employees and clinicians, but patients as well. Practice managers also try to further initiatives the DSO and clinical vision is pursuing. Helping practice managers succeed means offering general training in areas such as reading financial metrics, leading team members, and successfully supporting clinicians.

Regional managers are those who oversee the practice groups of their assigned region and support the practice managers and doctors. They are the coaches and coordinators between the DSO resources and the practice-level needs for support and leadership. They make sure, for instance, that practice managers get the resources to train and that HR is connecting practices with the right people. They ensure the practice managers feel supported by all the resources available at the DSO.

THE SECRET POWER OF THE PROJECT MANAGER

Here's a position you may not have heard much about. Project managers do not steer and manage people. Instead, they are in charge of leading strategic initiatives.

Imagine you are undertaking a strategy of specialty growth. One of your plans is integrating orthodontics into practices because your team has been referring out mega dollars in ortho every year. We know patients love one-stop shops, so you think this will be a great service.

Who is going to make it happen successfully? Will you just tell the practices, "We are now going to have all ortho referred in to our own orthodontists" and it will happen? Or will you announce, "All doctors will get trained in orthodontic treatments" and they will sign up and lead the team? Not likely.

Here is the place of great project managers: to assess opportunities, organize projects, align teams, and help in executing initiatives. We call this process IDOPE: Idea, Document, Organize, Prioritize, and Execute.

During your entrepreneur phase, you might have seen your ideas fizzle out or have had a rocky ride as they were implemented in your practice. Now you know why. You needed a dedicated project manager in your organizational chart.

No matter how brilliant an idea looks on a whiteboard or how critical it is for the business, without a clear and organized plan for execution, without all the appropriate resources prepared for the team to execute well, the idea will not happen.

The reality is that the bigger and better the idea is, the more likely it will require change management, an IT component, a compliance component, and a marketing component.

Instead of letting the idea fizzle out, a project manager takes charge of the idea, documents it, organizes it, prioritizes it (against all the other brilliant ideas), and puts together the resources to execute on it.

Any great idea usually requires a lot of analysis to determine the cost and value of implementation. After getting together with everyone involved, the project manager will go back to the executive to present the cost and the time and people needed to see the idea come to fruition.

The project manager's presentation allows the C-suite executives to make properly informed decisions on whether or not to go forward. And they learn what allocations and personnel they must okay to undertake the idea. The project manager and the C-suite work together to more clearly define the scope of the project, the resources needed, and the expected time frame for completion.

Once the project manager gets the go-ahead, they begin coordinating, bringing in specialists and the needed components to initiate and shepherd the project to completion.

Having someone dedicated to running with ideas can create a lot of strategic growth within your company. The top people can really focus on steering and vision. At the same time, the project managers protect the end users. They'll go to the practice manager and the team for feedback, asking, "What would be the challenge of having this new idea in your practices? What don't you have or what training do you need?" A practice is where the rubber hits the road in terms of execution, the *gemba* (a Japanese term meaning "the actual place or the location where value is created") where value arises for clients. Getting a bunch of feedback up front is crucial.

A good project manager builds their plan around those obstacles. By the time you finally roll out the new idea, everything needed will be in place. There will be a training system, those at the front desk will have a cheat sheet for things they need to know for the new clients, and so on. The entire practice will feel massively supported.

The project manager counters the traditional way that people function within an organizational chart and how they initiate projects. The traditional organizational chart often has an ivory tower feel to it. Someone in an ivory tower says, "I've got this brilliant idea! I want it done. It will do our business good!"

Meanwhile, the grand idea is completely disconnected from what's really happening at the ground floor: the challenges they're facing, the obstacles they have, and what they feel is most important to support what they need. *Gemba* represents all of that. Project managers go to *gemba*, connecting the visionaries up top with the realities on the ground. In that way, the business and everyone within it are aligned.

THE THREE GROUPS YOU NEED IN YOUR ORGANIZATION

I use a framework in building an organizational chart that I first heard from Dan Sullivan, founder of Strategic Coach. He explains that there are three types of team members you need within your organization:

1. Those who make it up

2. Those who make it real

3. Those who make it recur

Let's break these down.

The "Make It Up" Team Members

Those who make it up are entrepreneurial, the explorers and visionaries. They love the whiteboard, coming up with new visions and ideas to scribble down. These are the people who, if you tell them there's a ten-foot wall in front of them, will come up with twenty ways to get around it. Their natural instinct is to maneuver around a problem. They're the "out of the box" thinkers and often the ones who try to do too much too fast and so overwhelm their teams. At least they'll never be stuck.

The "Make It Real" Team Members

These are the liaisons and buffers. They take those whiteboard ideas from the "make it up" people and break them down into bite-size, easier-to-manage changes digestible for the "make it recur" people. They help to organize how to overcome obstacles to executing the vision and strategy. As liaisons and buffers, the "make it real" people rein in the visionaries while motivating the more singularly focused "make it recur" folks, who can help improve processes.

In real-world scenarios, you'll find "make it real" people creating FAQ pages, working with technology, and teaming up with an operations team to simplify a process. They'll document problems, determine processes, and package it all into a simple box that makes change management easier on everyone involved. This is the primary group I find missing from most organizations. We call them our project management team.

The "Make It Recur" Team Members

These people keep things going on a day-to-day basis. There isn't much variation in their work. They are single-tasked and focused, and that focus is often narrow. They bring value incrementally over time.

For example, the billing team sending out claims every day performs an activity without much variation. Likewise, the team members and staff who set up trays, sit next to you chairside, check people in, or take X-rays perform the same tasks every day. Their recurring job tasks also don't have much variation, and they often hate change coming down from the "make it up" people.

You might think that they're not good at coming up with new ideas. That's not their weakness, though. It's just that they hate change. Even incremental differences and improvements can feel exponentially large to them, and before you know it, too much change spins their day out of control.

Have you ever wondered why naysayers are always convinced something new won't work? These are the people who want everything to stay the same. New ideas disrupt their comfort zone, making them resistant to change.

What happens when "make it up" people interact with "make it recur" people? Well, they can drive one another nuts. So how do you get these two disparate types of people to come together? Add "make it real" people to the discussions.

The "make it real" people are a boon for you as well. Hiring "make it real" people who are adept at organizing and prioritizing frees you up to expand your recurring impact throughout the organization. It frees you up to look at your hires from a leadership point of view. And it frees you up to think about the future when you will move into a DSO to fulfill your vision with an executive team.

Bringing on executives provides its own special challenge, so we'll talk about that in the next chapter.

CHAPTER 11

Building Your Executive Team

There's a saying that goes something like this: a sliver of light between misaligned leaders can create a blinding light for everyone below.

In other words, alignment up top is critical to ensure that those below understand the vision of the company and are not left confused.

When I first hired executives, I didn't understand that alignment. Yes-men won't help their leaders grow or offer up hard-to-hear things, so I deliberately hired resistors instead of go-along people. I wanted to be pushed and challenged, to hear all sides of an argument, and I loved their dissenting voices. I loved the conflict and how they pointed out flaws. It made me think hard about how to take on challenges and grow.

It took a while before I realized something else was at play. Those dissenters didn't believe in the vision. Those challenging voices that drove me to do better didn't want to be on the team. To my surprise, they didn't even like the other team members.

What I needed were not people bent on arguing and personal conflict, people disinvested in the team and the company moving forward. What I needed were people of character, know-how, and experience who would call it as they saw it and who were aligned and invested in the common cause of best work and best practices. It was a hard lesson learned.

Below I will give you more details on common roles and responsibilities of executives, but the most important responsibilities executives have are supporting the vision of the company, upholding the culture, and helping ensure that the DSO is always focused on supporting the customer.

SCALING YOUR EXECUTIVE TEAM

As your company grows, roles will shift and evolve. You're still building, laying the groundwork for your matured business. It's normal.

In our first two years at Community Dental Partners, we went from twenty people in one location to more than two hundred team members. That's dramatic growth.

At the same time, my executive team was shifting and changing almost every four to six months. Why? Because who we needed in our first stage was different from who was needed for the second stage, the third stage, and so on.

As you grow, you'll also want to continually reassess whether those you've given an executive title are still the right people in the right positions or whether you need to make a change.

GAINING CLARITY BEFORE HIRING

Before you begin to hire an executive, it's important to get very clear on why exactly you need to hire. What needs, problems, issues, and created opportunities can this executive role solve or bring to your business? And, personally, what anxiety are you trying to relieve for yourself?

Documenting these is really important as a "hiring North Star." Once you're in front of somebody, you might be swayed by personality or their amazing résumé or the fact that they worked for a competitor. But your North Star reminds you what you're really trying to hire for and why. The right person might not be the most dazzling, but they're the solution you need right now.

The more detailed your North Star is, the better your chance of making the right hiring decision. Start listing out where you need help. You might write down something like "My financials are a mess. I need a better marketing strategy. I need help with HR. I'm concerned about my compliance."

When you step back and look at it, you might ask yourself, *Is there going to be someone who can figure out my IT issues and payroll system, make sure I'm clinically compliant, get my finances cleaned up, and be a better leader for my HR operational processes?*

The answer is no. We call this "hunting for a unicorn." But often people try to hire "the one perfect person." It doesn't matter if you give them the title of integrator or operator or executive, humans are only good at so much and can only take on so much. It's not fair to ask people to try to be a Swiss Army knife of executive capability.

Instead, the right hiring intention focuses on finding a strategist in a business specialty. The right person can strategically lead, and you will pay a lot of money for that leadership.

THE FOUR STEPS TO AN EXECUTIVE ORGANIZATIONAL CHART

I've given you a lot to think about. At this point, you might feel ill-equipped to do a good job. Let me provide you a way to transition into hiring an executive by steps.

Step 1: Join a Peer-to-Peer Networking Group

Joining a peer-to-peer networking group such as the Dentist Entrepreneur Organization gives you a place to network with others who are a bit ahead of where you're at. You can reach out with your questions and find answers and advice:

"Hey, I'm running into *x* issue. I'm thinking about hiring this [*title*] to help take care of it. Have you hired this [*title*]?"

They might come back and say, "Hey, I thought the same thing. You will want to look at this first" or "I found that solving *z* took care of my issue, so I didn't need to hire that person" or "Oh, yes—I hired [*title*], and, oh my gosh, it was everything I'd hoped for. Here are the attributes I looked for when I hired."

A peer-to-peer group can be a way to vicariously learn from all the mistakes others have made and avoid your own mistakes in the process.

Step 2: Hire a Consultant

Hiring outside help for certain functions may be a great solution for personnel gaps in your business or to free yourself of certain company duties. Maybe you hire someone to be a financial consultant. Maybe you hire an accounting firm and say, "Hey, could you help me with some of my CFO needs?"

You're going to ride these horses for as long as you can to avoid hiring until you're ready. In other words, you won't have to shoot for and hit the bull's-eye on a high-priced executive. Hiring outside consultants lets you see what does and doesn't work for you. Like dating, it helps you learn who you're really looking to settle down with.

And sometimes a consultant comes in and permanently solves some system or problem. Thank goodness you didn't pull the trigger on an executive hire you no longer need!

Step 3: Hire a Fractional Executive

Sometimes you strike gold with a consultant. Not only do you love them, but you also find they're bringing tons of value. You realize what they bring is something you could use on an ongoing basis. But you still don't have to jump to full-time executive yet. Instead, you can hire a fractional executive. Many consultants are willing to become your fractional executive, that is, they are willing to work part-time as an executive for your company. Typically, they work ten to twenty hours a week, but sometimes more.

In this situation, you're getting somebody a little more dedicated to your business than a consultant, specifically because they have a limited number of customers they'll take on as fractional clients. Meanwhile, this fractional relationship gets you strategic time from them. Now you have somebody who can show up to meetings with you, brainstorm new opportunities with you, or perhaps help execute longer projects.

Step 4: Hire a Full-Time Executive

The first three phases are a great way to get MBA-level know-how and experience in what you need and how your needs might be fulfilled—or not fulfilled. Moving through the phases positions you to hire full-time with less anxiety. Taking this final step is a natural fit when you need the big resources an executive can bring so that you can move your business to the next level, when the ten or twenty hours a fractional executive provides just isn't enough anymore, or when you've hired additional team members who need more leadership than the hours a fractional executive can provide.

EXECUTIVE HIRING ORDER

I often get questions about which executive should be hired first. Part of the answer comes from taking the time to consider who you truly need, your expectations for them, and how it will free you up for other areas of your business. In general, though, you hire executives in the order you need to evolve your business.

The first area of leadership needed is clinical leadership and vision. That began and continues with you. As you've hired clinicians, you have gradually come to think of yourself as an executive and are, in fact, the chief dental officer. You provide the vision for what your business does with its core competence: dentistry. You decide the capabilities you will provide to your patients and who those patients will be, both now and in the future. You create a standard of care and make sure that all clinicians coming on board know how to provide it.

With the clinician aspect covered, you turn to marketing because, as we discussed, marketing brings in the patients, and without patients, no other support positions are required. The CDO and CMO are tied to the revenue generation that paves the way for later hiring needs.

Your strength as a true CDO comes into play when you bring in a CMO because an energetic executive might approach you with opportunities for patients that are a mismatch for your business. If you cater to children, and the marketer presents a cool ad idea for dentures, you can't let yourself be persuaded into adding this new patient type. In fact, you won't be swayed if your vision is clear and you have plans in place to achieve it. If you aren't a strong CDO in your own right, strategic, high-powered, type A executives can overrun you. They are a fast-moving force. You must be the boundary that limits their reach.

In an orderly world, after hiring a marketing officer, your business evolution and growth would lead you to hire an operations officer, a compliance officer, and then a finance officer.

Operations and compliance assure fulfillment of your business offerings. Finance is about bringing increased clarity and understanding to your business.

But life doesn't move in a lockstep way and neither will your business. In reality, the five executive specialties might be served in different ways. You might have brought on a compliance officer early because you take Medicare and Medicaid patients. You might have continued serving as CDO, using your peer-to-peer network to get better at performing your role. Your early marketing consultants might have turned out to bring you a great patient flow with the resulting revenue generation. As you grew, you went from a fractional executive to a full-time COO who has brought order to all day-to-day workings throughout your practice locations. You finally take the leap to full-time CFO as you consider a greater expansion and seeking investment.

SETTING PROPER EXPECTATIONS

After hiring an executive, the natural expectation is that the executive will free up a bunch of your time. That won't happen. It will feel painful because, as I know from experience, we typically hire at the point of being overwhelmed. You want the executive to hit the ground running, but in the first thirty days, they can barely remember where the bathroom is, what your name is, and where the pencils are. Orientation takes time.

The best practice, generally, is to plan on losing time on the front end. To ensure their success, you must give an executive the time to explore their new environment, its culture, and those operating within it. Let them gain situational awareness before you expect them to free you.

A mistake I've made and have seen made is setting unrealistic expectations for the executive hired. High-caliber executives need to be coached to keep their powder dry when they come onboard. They are eager, and if you give the impression that they need to bring value immediately, they will do it—but at the expense of your culture.

They don't know where the land mines are. They don't know the nuances of the processes and systems of the company. They can't, without acclimation, understand the sophisticated ways of interaction and the communication practices, some of them silent and understood only with time. And they'll barge into all that like a bull in a china shop, trying to bring that immediate value that supports you, since you've brought them in to be a savior for your company.

I've seen executives who feel they must immediately perform get fired or walk out six months after being hired. It's because we didn't ease their landing into our company. High performers need to be coached to learn the culture first and bring value second.

A simple script I use when I hire someone is to tell them, "I don't expect you to bring any value for the first ninety days.

And it may take six months. What I really need you to do is learn about the company."

I have found that, of all the things we do for onboarding, just laying out that ninety-day to six-month time frame has been a great way to seed success. You get that same high-caliber individual, likely a type A personality, who is focused entirely on learning the company. They'll be thorough—learning about culture, understanding, decision trees, communication platforms, how decisions are made, hierarchies—they'll become expert observers, and they'll end up becoming fully integrated. Their success will increase dramatically.

THE EXECUTIVE ROLES

Here is a list of six common executive roles:

- Chief dental officer (CDO)

- Chief marketing officer (CMO)

- Chief operating officer (COO)

- Chief financial officer (CFO)

- Chief compliance officer (CCO)

- Chief technology officer (CTO)

Let's take a look at each.

Chief Dental Officer (CDO)

Your CDO is the clinical leader for the entire organization across locations. All departments need to be aligned with the CDO, who, in many ways, is more of a leader than the CEO.

What do I mean? Well, the DSO can't go faster than the clinical vision. You can't be out selling or creating products that the clinical team isn't willing or able to provide. This being the case, it's really important for the CDO to set the vision for the clinicians. In doing that, the CDO sets the vision for the whole company.

The CDO determines the clinical services to be provided, oversees the hiring process of clinicians, and does the clinical review of charts.

The CDO will often pull in dentists to form a clinical executive committee or team. The committee helps make clinic-oriented decisions such as suppliers and labs to be used and the next specialty to be added.

THE CDO'S REPORTS

The following positions report to the CDO:

- Clinicians

- Supply purchasing team

- Clinical recruiting team

- Operational teams tasked with a specific clinical initiative they want to improve

In addition to this clinical team's day-to-day roles, they may also interact with state boards, engage in government relation activities, manage compliance issues and complaints, and deal with legal and even insurance companies. The CDO is responsible for overseeing all of these people, processes, and details.

Chief Marketing Officer (CMO)

This role is often twofold, including sales and marketing. Sales and marketing increase patient flow by developing marketing campaigns, identifying brands, and knowing how to maintain brand consistency, all of which drive traffic to your business. In their role, they keep the customer's experience consistent and make sure any documents going out represent your brand.

Your CMO will work with doctors and practice managers to find niche markets that align with community needs and clinical capability. This helps ensure that services that make clinicians uncomfortable aren't being sold.

Ultimately, CMO focus is patient experience as well as patient flow. If the CMO's activities don't increase patient flow or improve patient experience, then their efforts are probably focused on the wrong things.

One of the most difficult things for your CMO will be explaining to the rest of the team the "why" of the projects they do. Not unlike the "make it up" people from last chapter, CMOs have to pressure-test their ideas (the project manager might help here). The "why" of their ideas—how putting up a billboard or gaining brand recognition through advertising in the paper, television, radio, or online will serve the DSO well—will not always be self-evident. It's up to CMOs to determine how to get the most bang for their buck in their marketing activities.

THE CMO'S REPORTS

The following positions fall under the marketing umbrella and report to the CMO:

- Graphic designers

- Media vendors

- Website developers

- Social media outlets or internal team members who focus on social media engagement (patients sharing their experiences with you on social media)

- Copywriters, individuals who write copy for websites, flyers, brochures, or blogs

These are the heart of your creative team. The most powerful CMOs I've seen are those who understand the customer better than anyone else in the organization does. The pain points alleviated most often by the CMO's team are getting patients in the door and finding someone who can manage patient experience by phoning patients to make, schedule, and confirm appointments.

As important as your chief marketing officer is, more often than not, the next position you'll likely want to fill is someone who can take care of people and system organization. Enter the chief operating officer.

Chief Operating Officer (COO)

Second only to the CEO, the COO helps to position the people and the company to present a unified front working on a single vision toward a common goal. They're always looking for opportunities to organize the business better and will work hand in hand with your CMO to help increase patient flow or improve the experiences of the patient and doctor. Concerned with both sides of the doctor–patient experience, the COO focuses their work on the systems and processes that make doctors' lives easier while improving patient experience.

COOs also work closely with the clinical director to ensure that any systems or processes put in place align with the clinical team's interests.

THE COO'S REPORTS

The COO oversees a wide variety of positions, including the following:

- Regional directors. The following people report to regional directors:

    * Practice managers and staff in recurring roles who see patients daily and implement relevant activities

    * Facility teams who manage the systems and processes of facilities

    * Human resources teams, crucially helping the COO manage the sheer number of people beneath them

The pain point alleviated most often by the COO is the inability to implement and execute actions to drive the business forward. If you don't feel ready for a COO, then you may consider bringing on an operations (ops) director as a midstep.

Your COO has a pulse on the company because of all the people they oversee. This focus on your people allows them to assess the health of your organization and determine how quickly projects can be implemented.

Chief Financial Officer (CFO)

The CFO can be one of the most difficult positions to hire because you need someone who appreciates the details needed to create accurate GAAP (generally accepted accounting principles) financial statements, can interact with investors and banks, and is a strategic leader with the executive team.

CFOs can be key in helping you build out your matrix and get your financial clarity nailed down. They are critical in decoding what financial documents say about your business. This is one of the pain points many businesspeople feel. For example, your CPA might be preparing financials for tax purposes but not for management purposes. What people hunger for in a CFO is someone who can organize the accounting figures in a way that gives perspective, clarity, and insight on how a business is doing from a management perspective.

In a DSO environment, the complexities intensify with multiple practices, holding companies, partners, and so on. Looked at this way, the CFO can be seen as a critical hire to ensure that cash flow, cash management, and accounting are clear between these various parties. The CFO has a lot of audiences they need to satisfy.

THE CFO'S INTERACTIONS

- Management team

- Accounting team

- Billing team

- Doctor-owners

- Banks

- Private equity firms

- Board members

There is a lot of interplay between departments for the CFO, and they must also manage their own teams focused on billing, cash flow, cash management, and accounting processes and systems. It's a role that requires wide arms.

Issues grow exponentially as you venture into multiple locations, DSO and sub-DSO structures, centralized resources, and a support center. The CFO can help roll out all financial information, providing different audiences with different levels of detail according to their needs. The CFO works with the management team to create budgets and forecast predictions, puts in accounting controls to make sure no one is stealing from you, manages payroll, and interacts with HR to include negotiating benefits with insurance companies, as well as seeing to the legal components of entities and bank account setups for cycle management of cash flow and projections.

With all this to get their arms around, it's important for a CFO to be able to orient on both big picture and deep detail.

Chief Compliance Officer (CCO)

In the healthcare industry, so many rules, regulations, and state and federal boards ensure a plethora of legal compliance that requires a dedicated officer as you scale and grow. That officer is the CCO. The CCO must ensure that everything is done according to the letter.

The CCO oversees all of the compliance and legal needs of your DSO business within the healthcare environment. At last count, there were approximately twenty-six different regulatory industries and agencies a CCO must monitor and comply with.

You're probably aware of a few of these, which come to mind immediately:

- OSHA

- HIPAA

- CMS

- HHS

- The State Dental Board

More than anyone else on the executive team, the CCO needs to understand the company vision at a level that helps them make good risk management decisions. Often, what the government or other regulators put out isn't black and white. The CCO can help protect your company against gray areas. The more aligned the CCO is with the team, the better they can help navigate their different responsibilities.

Ultimately, the role of CCO is to protect your business and the dentists' licenses so that the dentists can continue to practice and serve customers.

Chief Technology Officer (CTO)

Today's world runs on information technology and all the technical wizardry it entails. The CTO oversees it all. Hardware and software responsibility is more complex than you might imagine. A practice runs practice management software, possesses

X-ray machines that must be installed and connected to patient information within software, and needs new software and systems developed to improve operations and patient experience. Phone systems must be connected to call centers and billing teams. Onboarding and off-boarding of employees happens digitally. Servers and workstations must be kept running seamlessly so that business operations go forward quickly and predictably. All these fall within the scope of the IT department.

As a growing DSO, you'll likely expand to a number of practices in disparate locations in a county, and later a state. Your CTO will need to know how to set up networks so that they are all HIPAA compliant. These networks must, of course, function for all your teams every day. If a problem does arise, your practices should only have to make a single call to fix the issue.

Another increasingly urgent responsibility of your CTO is preventing security breaches. While no business is immune, it is critical to have the most up-to-date preventions in place, and, if a breach does happen, to solve for damage and regain control as quickly as possible.

Obviously, the CTO is critical in defending your business and stabilizing the connected technologies across your business to make things as efficient as possible.

With your six C-suite members in place, you've built a solid executive team who can help lead from their areas of strength whether you grow to ten, thirty, or even one hundred practices.

You've come a long way, but most dentist school graduates retain a hole in jargon that haunts them as they build their dental empire. We'll fix that in the next chapter.

CHAPTER 12

Knowing the Finance Jargon

Accounting and Financials

To close out the book, I wanted to introduce some terms that get thrown around that may help you as you interact with other business professionals and your finance team. Few of these were taught in our long years of education.

Brave dentist-entrepreneurs often ask us about these matters, so this chapter will give you some general basics to go on.

CASH-BASED ACCOUNTING VERSUS ACCRUAL ACCOUNTING

Cash-based accounting is easy enough to understand, since it's much like balancing your checkbook. Whatever comes in is recorded right away, and whatever goes out is likewise recorded. In an office, that means income minus expenses equals net income.

It seems so easy that most small businesses opt to use cash accounting. But it has some major drawbacks. For example, what I am calling revenue is actually the income from multiple months of production trickling in to the current month. What I am calling expenses are the bills I paid this month. Subtracting collections from previous months from expenses I paid this month actually tells you nothing about how your business is doing.

While your revenues are arriving in an irregular rhythm, the same is not happening in other areas of your books. Employees must be paid regularly. Your vendors and creditors expect the same.

In the months when your expenses fall like a hammer for quarterly payments, extra payroll, or double rent payments and your revenues are so featherlight that they don't even make a dent in what must go out, you might be tempted to make impulsive and imprudent emergency decisions with incomplete information. In fact, your business might be growing but just not collecting yet. This is hidden by the cash accounting method.

Or maybe your previous months were excellent for production, and now you are finally collecting the income and things are feeling great, but in actuality your production is falling apart. Cash accounting does not show this.

Cash-based accounting is great for businesses that have all expenses and income happening in the same month and aligning perfectly with one another. But anytime a business has production in one month and collections trickling in over the months ahead, the cash-based method of accounting can fall short.

The accrual method will give you additional clarity and management superpowers. Knowing the realities of each month as they happen will allow you to lead the organization with more accurate strategic thinking. Accrual accounting won't be as simple as balancing your checkbook, and it will mean hiring a CFO, as most CPA firms struggle to get this done. But the investment is well worth the return.

Here's an example of how accrual might look for a practice in a given month:

In accrual accounting, you look up the production for your current month. You would record this in your accounting ledger as gross revenue. You would then make journal entries in your ledger to offset how much of that you will actually collect. These adjustments are done by analyzing your historical adjustments, write-offs, and overall collection rates.

The first entry could be an adjustment percentage for the people you gave discounts to. The second entry could be a write-off percentage for the write-off of uncollected billings. The third entry could be for any finance plans you have given to patients you believe will not fully pay, called bad debt.

With a good CFO and revenue cycle management team, you'll get better and better at predicting what the write-offs, adjustments, and bad debt will be, giving you an increasingly accurate picture of your current month. Notice that you don't wait to record your revenue when it comes in. You record it in the month in which you earn it. This allows for real-time, accurate leadership of your practices. When you hear the terms *gross revenue* and *net revenue*, you are hearing the difference between revenue before all the adjustments and revenue after the adjustments. Net revenue is the amount you believe will be collected.

Now you'll look at expenses like rent and wages, understanding that these are real expenses for the month. Let's say you double-pay your rent because you paid for the current month on the first and you paid for the following month on the thirty-first. Your CFO will move the extra expense into its appropriate month rather than keeping it in the current month. This differs from the cash method, where both rent payments would stay in the same month.

If you owe insurance every quarter, your CFO will break it out over three months, so you can always be accurate on what the real numbers for the month are. All these little steps help bring clarity to your business's finances, and this will reverberate throughout your dealings with executives, management, banking, private equity, clinical partners, and other stakeholders.

The accrual method takes substantially more work to institute than the cash method. But it pays out in providing business intelligence for internal management and credibility to outside parties.

EBITDA

I pronounce EBITDA "ee-bid-da."

EBITDA is an acronym that stands for earnings before interest, taxes, dividends, depreciation, and amortization. Let's look at each component of EBITDA:

E (Earnings)—The net income of your practice or multiple practices consolidated.

B (Before)—Before the things about to come out of earnings, which make up the rest of the acronym.

I (Interest)—The interest you're paying on equipment or other loans acquired to establish your practice. This is added back to earnings.

T (Taxes)—We all understand taxes. This is added back to earnings.

D (Depreciation)—Fixed assets such as furniture, fixtures, and equipment (FFE) can't be expensed on your profit and loss (P&L) statement. They depreciate according to GAAP and tax code requirements. This depreciation number is added back to your earnings.

A (Amortization)—Similar to depreciation, amortization allows you to allocate a portion of a business you've bought toward fixed assets. The difference between your purchase price and those subtracted fixed assets must be booked somewhere. It's generally booked as goodwill on a balance sheet, which then has to be amortized over some period of time. This is added back to your earnings.

What this all comes down to is that EBITDA is a shortcut to look at the cash flow of your business. Most bank covenants and purchase transactions will be based on the EBITDA of the organization.

WHAT EBITDA IS NOT

It is *not* your actual cash flow. EBITDA is used as a comparison and for driving toward a valuation of your business. The only thing that represents your true cash flow is your actual cash flow, which is in a cash flow statement.

Remember, EBITDA stands for earnings before interest, taxes, depreciation, and amortization. The T stands for taxes, and you do actually have to pay taxes on your business.

If you have a loan that is amortized over a period of time when you're paying both interest and principal, both of those are excluded from EBITDA's calculation of cash flow. Without those, you can quickly see how far away from cash flow this EBITDA number is. It also does not account for any capital expenditures you need to make in your business. Buying new equipment, upgrading an office, and so on—none of this is included in EBITDA.

Now you understand why I say that EBITDA is the lazy person's shortcut to cash flow, but it's not cash flow. Just make sure you don't mix the two concepts as you grow your business.

It's always been fun for me to find the intelligence lurking in the numbers of my business. As you come to understand and implement more accurate financials, this understanding will bolster your leadership and confidence in your decisions.

Conclusion

I wrote this book to help dentist-entrepreneurs, wherever you are on your journey, learn how to get started on building your dental empires. The journey is hard and long. It takes hard work to learn, to gain experience, and to develop skills you never needed in dental school. If you've read this far, though, I know you are motivated to face any challenges that come your way. And they will come.

The industry has changed, but that has brought its own opportunity: the DSO. With a DSO, you can build a vision that supports the lifestyle you want while doing good by your community and your family. Giving you the secrets of the path is an honor for me. If you follow the path I've set out and continue to study and learn the concepts described here, you can get there.

First, though, you have to decide whether you really want to become a dentist-entrepreneur. It's not for everyone and it shouldn't be. The sacrifices you'll make to build a strong culture and successful business take away from other opportunities you don't have time to get to. Thoughtfully consider what your vision is and what you are or are not willing to give up and why. This is a crucial step before you go forward.

Going forward means becoming an ACE clinician. Your availability, capabilities, and engagement determine your ability to serve your customer with excellence. And you must train your associates to become ACE clinicians before transitioning into being an entrepreneur.

Becoming an entrepreneur means looking at your practice as a business. Your mindset must change from working in the business to working on the business. The practice is the foundation, so ensure it is sound in caring for your customers. This phase is a testing one because, as a business owner, you have to delegate and give up control.

Just when you seem to be getting the hang of it, you will hit the Dark Tunnel. It's a rite of passage, you must remind yourself. In the tunnel, you'll feel as if you're going backward and as if you may lose everything. Remember that you can reach out for help at our *DSO Secrets* podcast or Facebook page. There you'll find peers and mentors who have been through it. They know that the Dark Tunnel means you're about to jump to the next level. My team is always open to help as well at the website CDP.dental.

The next level, as you learned, is becoming an executive. Here you'll find a great bonus for hanging in there. As an entrepreneur, you're doing it right when you're putting in blood, sweat, and tears. If you're doing it right as an executive, scaling your business gets easier as you learn to depend on and develop your team. As an executive, you learn to prioritize your strategies and maximize your efforts.

You've also learned what a DSO is. It's not an evil entity. It is an organization that supports clinicians. You can partner with an existing DSO—and I've taught you what to look for—or you can build your own.

Either way, it all comes down to creating an amazing customer experience, and the customer you're catering to as a DSO is your pool of clinicians. Not only do you want to do your best to help them do their very best for the patients, you want to create the sort of workplace that attracts the best clinicians.

On the next leg of your march through the book, you learned the pros and cons of acquiring existing practices or building new ones. Weighing the considerations against your circumstances and existing skillsets will help you choose wisely.

Of course, then you'll need financing and investment. I've explained the banks' processes and different places to look for the funds to bankroll your dental empire dreams. You have definitely learned a lot, and when you reach this milestone in real life, you'll have come a long way.

Next we explored your organizational chart and the different layers of executives and middle management. I revealed that the secret of bringing vision to reality is the project manager. A project manager is the difference between ideas never seeing implementation and ideas changing the future of your business for the better of everyone.

At the beginning of your journey, you may have not even thought about what an executive does. At this stage, though, you need a clear understanding of the team you are going to lead in building your dental empire. You have learned the different roles and where they fit in an organization.

In the last chapter, I unshuttered the dark secret that is the Achilles' heel of our industry: our ignorance surrounding accounting and financials. You learned the uses and misuses of the term EBITDA. You also learned about the accounting method that will let you know what is happening in your business from the numbers in your ledgers.

As far as you've come, there are more things to discover. As you continue forward, you can meet like-minded dentist-entrepreneurs at various stages in their own journeys. Some can become your peers, some will mentor you, and you can become a mentor yourself. These new acquaintances can be found when you join DEO—the Dentist Entrepreneur Organization. I hope you do engage with our communities. Finding others who

know what it's like—the journey, its hardships, its triumphs—
others who speak your language, is so personally gratifying and
enriching.

I look forward to hearing about your failures and triumphs.

And until next time, *keep smiling.*

Reminder: In order to not bog down the book but still
provide you with multiple tools and video resources, I
have set up a website at DEOdentalgroup.com/dso-se-
crets/. You will see a QR code in several chapters that will
direct you to these resources.

Made in the USA
Las Vegas, NV
06 March 2023

68608727R00113